es in Cambridge New England

D Hollis   E Holden Chapel

P Revere sculp

JOSHUA COIT
American Federalist
1758–1798

JOSHUA COIT

American Federalist

1758 - 1798

BY

Chester McArthur Destler

WESLEYAN UNIVERSITY PRESS
Middletown, Connecticut

To My Mother

M. Louise Griesemer Destler

Contents

Preface

JOSHUA COIT was a New England gentleman who reached his majority during the American Revolution. After attending Harvard College he chose the law as his profession and public life as his career. He supported the new "Standing Order" of Connecticut. As a friend of Noah Webster, he contributed to the development of a federalist polity for Connecticut. This included the inauguration of commercial banking. In thought and statesmanship he typified the moderate liberalism of the era before the Reign of Terror in France precipitated a prolonged reaction. After achieving prominence as a legislator, he was sent to Congress in 1793.

Coit's Congressional career was significant nationally. He steered deftly between the Anglophiles and the Gallophiles, withholding admiration from the corrupt "British Constitution" and abhorring the term "Jacobin," which Jefferson had believed suitable in 1792 for his following. Coit was an American Federalist. He became an influential leader of the bipartisan moderates who held the balance of power in Congress between the major parties. He upheld the presidential treaty-making power. He opposed involvement in the wars of the French Revolution. Loyalty to the Federal Union led him to oppose the Northern secessionists who would disrupt the Union rather than submit to Southern control. This element was strong in Connecticut among the Federalists. Coit fought it on national issues at the risk of his political future.

In so doing he illustrated the continuance in American politics of the ideal of the legislator who voted as his judgment dictated rather than in strict adherence to "party." This practice derived immediately from *The Federalist* and remotely from the English country party of the previous century. Coit stressed American interests, necessities, and precedents. He refused at times to cater to the Administration. After an ill-conceived attack upon the contingent secessionists, he influenced the course of American history decisively during the X Y Z excitement of 1798.

I am especially indebted to the late Miss Gertrude E. Coit of New London, Connecticut, for making available without restriction Joshua Coit's letters to his wife and oldest son; to Robert S. Coit of Cambridge, Massachusetts, for making available without restriction Joshua Coit's letters to his brother Daniel Lathrop Coit and also a James Peale miniature of Joshua Coit; and to President Joseph A. Stanners of the Union Bank and Trust Company of New London for opening its manuscript archives, also without restriction. Dwight C. Lyman, President of the New London County Historical Society, has granted access to important manuscript sources. Special acknowledgments of similar courtesies are due to the Connecticut Historical Society, Connecticut State Library, Harvard University Archives and Library, New London Public Library, New York Public Library, and Yale University Library. Illustrations were supplied by Harvard University Library, the Library of Congress, Brooklyn Museum, and the Connecticut Historical Society.

I am indebted to my wife for constructive suggestions for the improvement of the manuscript.

CHESTER MCARTHUR DESTLER

West Hartford, Connecticut
November 1961

Introduction

THE United States in 1793 presented to Europe the picture of an immature, divided, sprawling republic whose weakness and indisposition to provide for its own defense invited intrigue if not aggression. Pre-democratic in the meaning of the "democracy" that was sensationalized by the Jacobin Club in France, the Americans were governed by an informal oligarchy of mercantile and landed gentry which included the clergy of the leading churches and successful members of the legal and medical professions. Upper officialdom on federal and state levels, together with veteran officers of the recent army of the War of Independence, also belonged to this ruling element. Unfortunately, this oligarchy was divided into bitterly hostile factions over the merits of a mercantile versus an agricultural policy and over whether or not to observe the provisions of the Franco-American Treaty of Alliance of 1778. Implementation of the treaty would have drawn the United States at once into the spreading War of the First Coalition against the French Republic and its allies upon the side of the latter, whose sea power was inadequate to defend either its own commerce or that of the United States from the powerful navy of Great Britain.

Despite the great name and presidential leadership of George Washington, the spreading fires of political warfare on national and state levels threatened to undermine the unity that he had achieved during 1787–1789 in the creation of the Federal Union with the aid of the patriot party of the Revolution. The swift dissolution of the one-party régime that he had established was preparing turbulently for the two-party alignment which has characterized the

American system ever since. Everywhere the divided American oligarchy was being challenged from below by the unenfranchised admirers of the Jacobins and their sans-culotte following. The position of the pro-French landowners was happier because of their intellectual rapport with the Gallophile mobs of the few cities and larger towns and with the equally Gallophile poorer farmers. Fear lest social upheaval and the guillotine be introduced into the United States by such turbulent elements acerbated the Gallophobia of the mercantile oligarchs and their allies. Almost in self-defense, as well as in behalf of their economic interests, this element looked to Great Britain.

There was real danger that the apple of discord tossed into American politics by the French goddess of Liberty would divide the United States into openly warring factions. This was evident to shrewd observers who watched the thinly masked intrigues of successive French Ministers, who were attempting to create a French party committed irrevocably by ideology and interest to the service of the French Republic. Holland and Switzerland, as the Batavian and Helvetian republics, provided contemporary parallels of ominous portent.

What was needed in this circumstance, from the standpoint of American national interest, was the cultivation of a moderate statesmanship that would bridge the widening gap between the embittered factions, which were already evolving into national parties. Moderation could cultivate the national interest and foster best the legitimate interests of commerce, industry, and commercial agriculture, thus pulling the divided country together.

Into this situation in 1793 there stepped a young Connecticut Congressman of moderate disposition who dedicated his talents to such leadership. Named Joshua Coit, he originated from an influential shipbuilding and mercantile family of eastern Connecticut which had been prominent in the American revolutionary movement almost from its beginning. By virtue of this, his Harvard

College education, and his standing in the legal profession and in the emerging banking community, he had been able to aspire successfully to membership in Connecticut's ruling "Standing Order." His distinguished service as an ally of Noah Webster in the Connecticut legislature, his elevation there to Speaker of the House of Representatives in 1793, and his election to Congress in October 1793 brought him within that one-party oligarchical circle. When he rode to Philadelphia that autumn as a new Congressman, he went as a representative of the alarmed Standing Order which sought to bulwark the federal government as a means of safeguarding society itself from Jacobinism.

Coit in 1793 was, of course, the product of his family background, regional origins, and successful career before the bar and in politics. The extent to which all this and his education had equipped him for the role of moderate statesmanship must now be ascertained.

JOSHUA COIT
American Federalist
1758–1798

CHAPTER ONE

A Young Gentleman of New London: Harvard 1776

"Sund 7 Mr. Byles pr al day. Capt. Joseph Coit a Son baptised Joshua," wrote Joshua Hempstead of New London, Connecticut, in his famous diary during the evening of October 8, 1758.[1] The diarist was approaching the end of his career when Captain Coit's newborn tenth and last child was brought into the community of the First Church of Christ, Congregational. The entry attested to the Captain's importance in that congregation and the town.

New London then comprised a thinly settled area including modern New London, present-day Waterford to the west and north, and modern Montville farther up the Thames River's west bank. A cluster of shops and houses sprawled on the gentle slope behind the wharves on the west shore of the inner harbor near the mouth of the Thames. The town's population was slightly more than 3000, consisting chiefly of New Englanders to which several hundred Indians and almost as many Negroes were added. Theirs was a modest total for Connecticut's only official port of entry under the British Navigation Acts.[2]

Captain Coit's was among the more conspicuous displays of merchandise imported from Great Britain, France, the Mediterranean countries, Boston, and the West Indies. His cousins, likewise descended from John Coit of Gloucester, Massachusetts, who had come in 1651 with others to found the town and the First Church, were important locally and in Groton across the harbor. Among the New London Coits was Dr. Thomas, for thirty years the leading physician. Justice of the Peace and innkeeper Daniel Coit, like the

Captain, was prominent in civic affairs and the First Church. The Coits' importance as a group of interrelated families almost rivaled that of the Shaws, Saltonstalls, and Perkinses.

During 1744 Captain Coit had headed the committee that petitioned George II for adequate fortifications for New London. During 1766 he had served on the First Church's pastoral committee. In 1758 he was a manager of the lottery authorized by the General Court to finance the erection of the lighthouse on the west bank of the entrance to the harbor. In December 1767, with Daniel Coit, he would be elected to the non-importation committee that cooperated with Boston in opposition to the Townshend Acts.[3]

Captain Coit was a member of a local shipbuilding family which for more than a century had built the largest vessels launched on the Thames, competing successfully with the Boston shipyards. As a youth he had begun an apprenticeship in ship carpentry in Boston, the commercial capital of New England. Dissatisfied after a short period there, he had returned to complete his training in New London. After experiencing a foot injury, he had gone to sea and had risen rapidly to master. After eleven successful voyages, he had settled down as a sedentary merchant in New London, sending his vessels as Captain Nathaniel Shaw did his to the West Indies with Connecticut horses, tub butter, salted fish, salt, cattle, tobacco, staves, lumber, barreled flour, pork, and beef, selling the smaller craft with their cargoes when they arrived at Kingston, St. Christopher, and Trinidad. Other vessels exchanged West Indian molasses and sugar at Boston for locally manufactured woolens and spermaceti candles, and for European wares, "sundry goods," books, cutlery, and wines. These supplemented merchandise brought directly from London and Bristol or smuggled in from France and the Mediterranean countries in customary defiance of the Navigation Acts.[4]

As the youngest of the Captain's eight living children, Joshua enjoyed the boyhood of a prominent merchant's son. His playmates were found among his cousins, the sons of other merchant families such as the Hallams and Stewarts and the recently arrived Gibsons from Edinburgh, the Thompsons and Allens, and the children of local lawyers and craftsmen. Ship arrivals and departures, the coastwise trade with the Connecticut River valley, Providence, Newport, and Boston, and the stagecoach on the post road kept the horizon broad. Contacts with the hinterland's farmers and with the fishermen, shipyards, and skilled craftsmen of New London and Norwich, where Joshua visited relatives, introduced him to the economic life of eastern Connecticut. Smuggling and defiance of the Townshend Acts instilled a love of liberty there. Household chores brought him into close touch with the domestic industries whereby his mother, his sisters, and the maids produced woolen and linen cloth, soap, and candles, while he learned to tend and milk the family cow, bring in the wood, and lay fires.[5] As he grew older, he was put to work in his spare time at his father's warehouse and stores when he was not attending school.

Young Joshua soon became acquainted with the region's religious pluralism, which was beginning to weaken the Congregational Church's official monopoly. He sat with his family in the First Church on Sundays, increasingly aware of the prestige and power that its members enjoyed in Connecticut's political and social life. In the First Church the influence of the port had modified the starched piety of its founders. Easygoing Reverend Mathew Byles Jr. permitted the Half-Way Covenant to displace the religious orthodoxy of the mid-century's Great Awakening. The chief excitement was supplied by irregular invasions of the First Church's services by the recalcitrant Quaker-Baptist Rogerenes during 1764–1766. They disrupted the services to the disgust of the deacon and congregation, suffered jail sentences in punishment, and precipitated attempts to repress them with tarring and feathering. More sensational if not more shocking to the First Church was the Reverend Mr. Byles' resignation in 1768, when Joshua Coit was ten years old, to accept the call of the Anglican North Church in Boston.

Possibly Byles' desertion to the Church of England was related
to the previous winters' visits of H. M. S. *Cygnet.* Its officers had
enlivened New London and outraged the devout with their tavern
and shipboard parties, sleighing, hunting, and public consorting
with the fair sex between seasons of coastwise searching for Yankee
smugglers.[6] The enthusiasm with which New Londoners supported
the non-importation agreement was related more to the *Cygnet's*
efficiency than to its officers' worldliness.

Increasingly serious studies, chores, and work for his father
filled most of Joshua's years before 1772. During 1770–1771, as he
became aware of the world of affairs and met such New London
notables as Richard Law, the leading lawyer, and Nathaniel Shaw
Sr., the leading merchant, the lad was strongly influenced by the
First Church's new pastor, the young Reverend Ephraim Woodbridge. Probably that clergyman was preparing him for college as
the pastor of Lebanon had trained Jonathan Trumbull, the great
inland merchant.[7] In the First Church the zealous Woodbridge
abruptly terminated the Half-Way Covenant's practice of admitting
teen-agers and adults to membership upon renewal of their baptismal
covenant. The new pastor insisted—in defiance of the congregation
and the First Ecclesiastical Society, which paid his salary—that a
candidate for membership exhibit religious zeal and the renewing
grace of the Holy Spirit, confess his faith before the congregation,
and present convincing evidence of a change of heart and conduct.[8]

From Woodbridge the thirteen-year-old Joshua learned Congregational orthodoxy and otherworldliness. He developed an almost
ecstatic religious zeal. These he expressed in October 1771 to an
older sister who lived in Norwich, in a letter describing God's plan
of redemption via the eternal Holy Trinity whereby He had given
His only Son to suffer and "dye for us," assuming thereby the guilt
of human sin in conformity with the "law of God." He continued:

> O! in consideration of these important things how mean do all the
> things of the World appear, an Interest in the precious merits of the

Lord Jesus Christ how vastly preferable is it to all the things of this World! Then let us set our affections on things above & not on things below, & Let us grow in Grace & in the knowledge of our Lord Jesus Christ. O May a sense of the great uncertainty of life engage us to continual Readiness for the important hour of Death, which we know must come . . .[9]

Timidity may have prevented him from applying for church membership at that time. Such a religious attitude suggested that the lad might find a suitable profession in the ministry, as had his great-uncle the Reverend Joseph Coit, Harvard 1697 and Yale 1702, the first pastor of Plainfield.[10]

Joshua Coit was prepared carefully for college in the hope, possibly, that as the favored youngest son he could win admission into the "Standing Order" of ruling families and successful men in Connecticut, as had Governor Jonathan Trumbull.[11] His example may have attracted the youth to Harvard College instead of to the more conservative Yale College, where Dr. Ezra Stiles, friend of Benjamin Franklin, was President. James Otis and John Adams, other leaders in the colonial resistance to British encroachments, were Harvard graduates also, while nearby Boston was the exciting center of that recurring agitation.

How well Coit was prepared for college became apparent when he applied for admission to Harvard in 1772. He passed the entrance examination by demonstrating his ability to translate "Greek & Latin Authors in common use, such as Tully, Virgil, the New Testament, Zenophen [*sic*], &c., his understanding of the Rules of Grammar," and his ability to "write Latin correctly." His references had certified to his "good moral character." [12] After this he was briefed on the college rules. These required that he attend morning chapel and evening prayers, and devote himself to religious "Duties" during the strict Sabbath from sundown Saturday to Sunday night. These duties included attendance at the Congregational Church, since he did not apply for permission to attend the Church of England.[13] He was the only Connecticut youth in the class of 1776, which was otherwise comprised entirely of Massachusetts young men.

Harvard was the leading colonial college. As Burnaby's *Travels in North America* had remarked in 1770, it was organized "not upon a perfect plan, yet has produced a very good effect." [14]

In Harvard Yard stood Massachusetts Hall, Hollis Hall, Stoughton Hall, and the smaller Holden Hall, together with the new chapel. John Hancock had contributed £500 to the recently revived library, after endowing the Hancock Professorship of Hebrew and Other Oriental Languages. The faculty consisted of the president, three endowed professors, and six tutors. Among them the most eminent was John Winthrop, Hollis Professor of Mathematics and Natural Philosophy. The tutors bore chief responsibility for instruction and supervision of the undergraduates, whose good behavior was supposedly ensured by an elaborate system of fines for tardiness at and absence from religious, class, and declamation exercises, and for failure to remain at their studies in "Chambers" at specified hours. [15]

The course of study had broadened significantly since the decades when it had been designed primarily for education of the clergy. While still predominantly classical, it was now relieved by attention to science, belles-lettres, and rhetoric while imparting some knowledge of theology.

Three tutors were assigned to a class, each instructing it "in rotation" for an entire week thrice daily from Monday to Thursday in his specialty. This was either Latin, or "Logic, Metaphysics, Ethicks," or "natural Phylosophy, Geography, Astronomy, & the Elements of the Mathematicks." The junior and senior sophisters declaimed "in the Chapel in one of the three learned Languages" in rotation. The junior sophisters were required to "dispute publicly once a Week through the Year" in the presence of the seniors and their tutors or professors. Each month the two upper classes held a disputation "in the Forensic Manner" between equal numbers speaking alternately upon a subject named by their tutor "at least a

Fortnight beforehand." On Friday mornings the "Freshmen and Sophomores" declaimed or more often listened to readings of "some celebrated Oration, Speeches, Dialogues in Latin or English" for the improvement of "their Elocution & Pronunciation." On Saturday mornings the tutors instructed their classes "in Theology, Elocution, Composition, Rhetoric & the Belles Letters." From this the senior sophisters were excused after spring vacation, possibly to prepare their commencement orations.

The "Disputations" evinced the continuing influence of the curriculum of the medieval universities, but their bias was now almost as much toward public life and the law as toward the ministry. In each of these professions a knowledge of classical examples, mastery of the ancient languages and literatures (except Hebrew, which was pre-clerical), and competence in speaking and debate were essential. That science received so considerable an emphasis was indicative of the influence of the eighteenth-century Enlightenment.

The four-year course was required for graduation with the bachelor of arts degree. In addition, each candidate had to demonstrate his ability "to translate the Old and New Testament into the Latin tongue," exhibit a "good acquaintance with the classics," display a command of "the principles of Mathematics, of Natural and Moral Philosophy, of Logic and Rhetoric," be "of an unblemished life," and give a satisfactory public performance before "the President and Fellows."[16] Although the belles-lettres were not included in these requirements, instruction in them had an indubitable appeal to youthful minds alert to the intellectual currents of the epoch. It made the remainder of the curriculum more palatable.

For some years the undergraduates had been strongly influenced by the Enlightenment with its exciting emphasis upon science, reason, criticism, and intellectual freedom. Deism was popular among the students, derived as it was from John Tillotson, Samuel Clark, Voltaire, and other religious rationalists. They maintained that God was a benevolent, rational, but remote scientific Deity. Rational religion received special recognition on the campus in the annual Dudleian Lecture. Paralleling a similar trend in England, deism spread widely among the Congregational clergy and lay leadership of Massachusetts' coastal counties and into Connecticut, according to Ezra Stiles' *Diary,* there challenging the tradition of the Great Awakening. At Harvard it was certain to diminish Joshua Coit's attachment to orthodox Congregationalism.

A broad interest in science also characterized the undergraduates, as it did educated adults along the seaboard. Professor Winthrop's discoveries in astronomy and geology, and his collaboration with Franklin in electrical experiments, combined with his lectures and demonstrations to give science special prestige in the Yard. Instruction in mathematics, including the calculus, evinced Sir Isaac Newton's influence and reinforced conceptions of natural law and rationality. In the library, *The Philosophical Transactions* of the Royal Society enabled Winthrop and his students to keep abreast of scientific developments in Europe.

The library stimulated also an interest in belles-lettres and political theory. Students read there the poetry of John Donne, Milton, Herrick, Edmund Spenser, Sir Philip Sidney, and Alexander Pope, together with Shakespeare's plays. Joseph Addison's *Cato* attracted some. Jean Jacques Burlamaqui's *Law of Nature* (*Principes du droit naturel,* 1747) and *The Spectator,* together with Joseph Addison and Pope, focused attention upon eighteenth-century thought. As the only textbook studied in political science, Burlamaqui brought students into tune with colonial Whig doctrines of natural and constitutional law. It made the study of classical republicanism especially suggestive. Plutarch's *Lives,* Demosthenes' and Cicero's *Orations,* Plato's *Dialogues,* and Aristotle's *Politics* seemed fraught with implications for contemporary problems to students fired by the rhetoric of James Otis and Dr. Joseph Warren, another Harvard alumnus among the colonial leaders.

The students read many of these treatises on their own initiative as well as for class recitations. Voluntary self-training was organized by secret student societies. The earliest and longest-lived of these was the Speaking Club, founded in September 1770. It was rivaled for a few years by the Mercurian and Clintonian societies. Shortly after Coit entered Harvard College, the Speaking Club absorbed the Mercurian, which was led by Fisher Ames. The enlarged society's members declaimed classical orations and spoke on themes related to "tyranny," "Liberty," the advance of science, and colonial opposition to Governor Thomas Hutchinson of Massachusetts and to Parliamentary measures.

Thus Coit's student generation enjoyed a dual program, curricular in the classroom and voluntary in the secret societies, which prepared Harvard men for public leadership by the study of antique republican cultures, modern science, and natural-law political theory. Almost before the students' eyes, the colonial committees of correspondence were putting the last-named into practice in 1772 as they assumed the practical business of government locally and in the province outside of Boston.[17]

The College was identified as early as 1770 with the colonial cause, of which Professor Winthrop was an influential leader. The General Court's meetings in the chapel during 1770–1773 had enabled Otis and Warren to address the students before its portico after the Boston Massacre in thrilling expositions of liberty with fruitful classical allusions. There developed also an interest in military tactics that produced the Marti-Mercurian Band, an elite company which recruited threescore members after April 1771 and contributed six to the minute-men in 1775.[18]

The undergraduates' passion for "Liberty" focused naturally upon arbitrary aspects of the College's administration. After a "liberty tree" was erected in the Yard in protest against imagined tutorial oppression, enforcement of the rules was relaxed by President Locke. Then his abrupt resignation was followed by a six-months' interregnum while the Corporation shopped for a successor. Samuel

Chandler, son of a revered Gloucester clergyman, filled his diary at that time with references to absences from chapel, recitations, prayers, and the campus also during his repeated visits to Boston. However, quarter bills for accumulated fines imposed upon others for such derelictions indicated a continued attempt to enforce traditional regulations.[19]

Since no such fines were imposed upon Joshua Coit, according to the "Records of the College," his conduct must have been exemplary. Quiet industry and cooperation with tutors and professors foreshadowed salient aspects of his adult character of later years. In May of his freshman year he wrote to his sister, Mrs. Lucy Huntington of Norwich, Connecticut, that he continued "to like College very well." Nothing could be "more delightfull" than to have all "my time to lay out in improvement of my Mind!" He was impressed with "the importance of time. *Moments seize—heavens on their wing.*" Undoubtedly he shared Nathaniel Walker Appleton's dismay at President Locke's mysterious resignation, the College's humiliation when Professor Winthrop and then two others refused the presidency, and concern at the long delay before Dr. Samuel Langdon of Portsmouth, New Hampshire, was inducted into that office "privately" on October 14, 1774, after the royal government had been overthrown in all Massachusetts towns not occupied by British troops. Coit stood in the Yard with the undergraduates that afternoon to receive the new President as he was accompanied to the chapel by the "Professors, Tutors & Graduates" for prayers. Langdon made "an extempore [English] Speech adapted to the Occasion, and the Service concluded with an anthem by the Undergraduates." [20] Eleven months later Coit heard him deliver the Dudleian Lecture.

During 1774 the burgeoning spirit of American Whiggery led for the first time to the cataloguing of students at Harvard College alphabetically, after the example set by Yale in 1769, rather than according to their families' social station.[21] Within a year the "mag-

nificent" Boston Tea Party—as John Adams termed it—had provoked the Boston Port Bill, the enlargement of the city's British gar-
rison, the appointment of General Thomas Gage as governor of
Massachusetts, and Parliamentary revision of the charter of that
colony. In reply to this attempt to crush colonial resistance, Rhode
Island rallied the colonies to Massachusetts' support, to universal
non-importation and non-exportation, and to joint action in a Continental Congress. Trade with the mother country was at a standstill
when Coit returned overland to Harvard College that autumn before Langdon's induction into office.

At breakfast on March 1, 1775, Coit joined the patriotic students'
attack upon the drinkers of "India Tea," smashing their teapots and
cups as symbols of disloyalty to America. The mild reprimand ad-
ministered that evening by Langdon's administration, which had
decided to forego the summer commencement in protest against
the Intolerable Acts and Gage's administration, indicated where
the College's sympathies lay.[22]

On April 19 Coit stood among the nine undergraduates remaining on the campus during spring vacation who met Lord Percy's
regulars with professions of ignorance of the road to Concord and
the minute-men's military stores there. They then spoke their scorn
of Tutor Isaac Smith, who pointed to the proper highway. They
welcomed the farmer minute-men as they swarmed into the Yard to
post themselves at coigns of vantage against Percy's return. Seven
months earlier, a British column had carried away two fieldpieces
from Cambridge. Now, after Percy returned to Boston by a more
direct route, the minute-men called on "Tory Row" on Brattle Street,
silenced its influential protest against embattled Whiggery, and returned to the Yard to remain in partial occupation of the buildings.

On May 1 Coit was sent home with the other undergraduates by
the Committees of Safety. Whereupon the Massachusetts Provincial
Congress requisitioned the College to house the gathering troops
and to serve as headquarters for the siege of Boston.[23] On July 16,

because of "the distressed & dispersed state of the College," the faculty remitted all recent punishments.[24]

Coit had joined the Speaking Club eighteen months earlier, during the autumn of his sophomore year, with Samuel Sewall of Boston, a classmate who would serve with him in Congress before becoming chief justice of Massachusetts. Both signed the "Declaration" pledging them "not to disclose any secret" of the Club and "to promote" its "best interest." Coit mastered its elaborate procedure, began to participate in its debates in the English language, and read the treatises on elocution that the critics' committee loaned to members. He became chairman of the committee on "extraordinary meetings." In June and again in November 1774 he was secretary *"pro tempore."* Finally, on December 12, 1775, he was elected secretary, the Club's chief executive officer.

During those years his share of the recorded programs cultivated a broad range of interests. Shortly after joining, he declaimed "part of Cicero's 2d Oration against Cataline," an oblique thrust at Governor Hutchinson. On December 14, 1773, he delivered "The Speech of Junius Brutus on the Death of Lucretia" on a program with Sewall, who declaimed "an extract from Pope's Essay on Man." During the following spring and summer, Coit declaimed extracts from two other Cicero orations, and spoke "On Poetry," "On Eloquence," and "On Society" from the small rostrum in the private home where the Society had a room. In September 1773, after being "punished for not speaking," he and Christopher Gore, another classmate and a future United States Senator, presented the "Dialogue between Narva and Massinissa." On December 13 he declaimed the moving "Speech of Socrates in Defense of Himself."

Especially indicative of his attitude toward the contest between the Continental Association and George III was Coit's original oration presented to the Club a fortnight before Lexington and Concord: "The Speech of a free Negro to the revolted Slaves in the West Indies." This was an early expression of the antislavery attitude of the American Whigs as they approached the War of Independence.

The Club's activity diminished in Coit's senior year, during which he spoke only twice on its programs. In mid-November he presented an "Extract from Goldsmith's Essays," duplicating Sewall's interest in contemporary belles-lettres. In late March 1776, with an original composition titled "Temple of Pleasure a Vision," he concluded the brief recorded programs of the year. In all his performances before the Club he avoided the scientific subjects that interested Gore. Instead, the American cause, intellectual freedom, rhetorical and social grace, belles-lettres, and "The Social Order" comprised the range of Coit's interests.[25] Obviously, he was socially ambitious.

His college class was permeated by a restive spirit of liberty that resisted onerous requirements. On March 31, 1775, three weeks before Lexington, the faculty granted its petition for relief from one of the three daily recitations in logic because "it is not expedient" to hold the class to the full curriculum.[26] The diminishing activity of the Speaking Club during 1775-1776 indicated the difficulties under which the College labored.

Perhaps 125 students had repaired on October 4, 1775, to Concord, whither the College had removed after "several Months in an interrupted & dispersed State" because of "the present War into which the American colonies have been driven to save themselves from Oppression & Despotism," as the faculty "Records" state. The faculty and librarian labored with local friends in Concord to improvise a reading room stocked with some of the library's books and apparatus. The students were removed from the taverns to private residences, some at such a distance that daily recitations during the winter quarter were reduced to two. These were held in the "Meeting House, Court House, & School House," which were improved "for the purposes of the Worship, Instruction &c of the College." Professor Stephen Sewall, Hancock Professor, taught the freshmen "in his room for a season" because of Tutor Smith's absence in England. Winthrop's and Sewall's lectures to the senior sophisters were continued on a revised schedule. Because of a text-book shortage, duplicate sets of Burlamaqui and of Gravesend's *Philosophy* were loaned to the students by the library. A faculty com-mittee labored to bring the remainder of "the apparatus, Philosophy Room, Library & Museum" from the Yard to Concord to sustain the curriculum. The numerous absences and late arrivals during the autumn because of the "perplexity & uncertainty at that time attend-ing the state of public affairs" were excused by the faculty.[27]

The College was financially embarrassed by its inability to collect rents from its properties and the now suspended Charlestown ferry. After an honorary doctorate of laws was conferred on General George Washington because he had driven the British army from Boston, outspoken student dissatisfaction with the dispersed and cramped quarters at Concord forced President Langdon's hand. Simultaneously, the Continental army's evacuation of Harvard Yard left behind buildings stripped of interior woodwork, brass doorknobs, and half a ton of lead. The damages, totaling £450, were beyond the College's ability to repair. John Hancock, the treasurer, was absent attending the Continental Congress.

However, President Langdon and the Fellows persuaded the General Court to order the College's return to the Yard on June 21. This allayed student discontent by making available "the benefit of the Apparatus," which the undergraduates regarded "as one of the greatest privileges of the Society." Since graduation was near, the faculty empowered the President to allow any senior sophisters "to go Home," although they had not "the benefit of the Apparatus." However, for those who remained and for the other classes the faculty extended the summer term to August 14, so that Professor Winthrop might present "his Experimental lectures (a very im-portant branch of their education)." The "retrieving" of the science instruction was advanced further by acquisition of the *Philosophical Transactions* for 1774. Then, after deciding against a "public Commencement this year" because of "the difficult & unsettled state of our public affairs," the Corporation awarded "a general diploma" to those nominated by the faculty for the bachelor of arts and master of arts degrees.[28]

Thus, whether or not Coit remained voluntarily to observe Winthrop's scientific demonstrations and to participate in experiments under his supervision, he graduated at Cambridge with the forty-three members of the class of 1776 on August 8 after paying the President's fee.[29] Despite interruptions and handicaps, he had completed his formal education as an American gentleman before he was eighteen years of age. He returned to New London wearing the dress and intellectual garb of an American patriot, imbued with the idealism and loyalties of the emerging spirit of nationality, and sharing the faith of the New England deists. Significantly, the inclusive catalogue of Harvard College classes published in Boston after his graduation was dated "Annoque Reipublicae Americanae primo." [30]

His leadership in the Speaking Club had pointed him unmistakably toward public life. For this, as the prominence of attorneys in the revolutionary movement indicated, legal training was almost indispensable. He chose the law as his profession. Such was Harvard College's immediate influence upon his life.

He studied law between 1776 and 1779, apparently in New London while working in his father's mercantile business. Possibly he read law with Richard Law, now a Connecticut delegate to the Continental Congress, during that notable's vacations in the town. Early in 1779 he was in Philadelphia at work in a minor capacity in the office of the paymaster of the Board of War. He hoped because of that dignitary's friendship for a more important post with an "increase in pay." When that failed to materialize he returned home. Coit was admitted to the bar later in the year, when he formed a partnership with shrewd but unpretentious Jeremiah Gates Brainerd, another young native son.[31]

Although Coit's father continued to reside in Norwich, to which he had removed his headquarters in 1775 after the battles of Lexington and Concord to escape British naval raids, Joshua remained in the inadequately fortified port. He returned to the First Church, but according to surviving incomplete records he did not offer himself for membership. He belonged to the First Ecclesiastical Society. Family tradition insists that he was also a member of the congregation. The Society supplied the Church with preachers until the Reverend Henry Channing was called as the next pastor in May 1787.[32]

Between 1776 and 1784 Coit's activities were confined almost entirely to eastern Connecticut. That region's prominence in the Revolution in Connecticut was attested by the leadership of Governor Trumbull, the Huntingtons of Norwich, and the Shaws and Richard Law of New London. Together these men rivaled the influence of the bitter promoters of the Susquehanna Company. Prominent among those men, other than Governor Trumbull, were three sons of ex-Governor Roger Wolcott. These included Oliver Wolcott Sr., of Litchfield.

Coit's initial success at the bar was intimately related to the fortunes of New London. The town grew rapidly under the stimulus of privateering and periods free from blockade. Whereas in 1776 streets extended but two to three blocks inland from the Embankment along the shore, and hardly more than four blocks north and south from The Parade with its outmoded battery facing the waterfront below the Groton ferry, by September 5, 1781, before General Benedict Arnold's raid struck the town, it had expanded noticeably. A printing shop was situated then north of the town mill amid a sprinkling of houses on the Norwich road. Houses, warehouses, and piers had been erected on Winthrop's Neck, previously bare, across Winthrop Cove from the customs house, mechanics' shops, warehouses, lumberyards, wharves, shipping, and ferry slip on the slope and shore north of The Parade from Water to Richards Streets.

The First Church and prominent residences were situated on Main Street, which ran north parallel with the shore and two blocks inland. Facing The Parade on the north were the courthouse, jail, Episcopal church, and shops. Crowding the shore and Embankment south of The Parade were shipyards, spar yards, ropewalks, piers with craft being outfitted, and the shops of subsidiary industries. Above that area, running south from The Parade paralleling the shore, was Bank Street. On it were situated large stores, warehouses, and intervening residences. Extending inland from The Parade up State Street were lesser shops, inns, and dwelling houses. Nathaniel Shaw's stone mansion and office was four blocks south from The Parade, a few feet inland from Bank Street. The stone Huguenot House and the large early wooden Hempstead House three hundred yards inland to the northwest of it had for years marked the edge of the best residential area away from the shops. Individual houses had appeared on the hill along the Colchester road to the west of the town burial ground, which was situated above Nathan Hale's schoolhouse, north of The Parade and overlooking the harbor from the west.

The elimination of the Loyalists from public life, association with his father's patriotic trade, and legal business incidental to privateering and disposal of the Tory estates furthered Coit's success at the bar. Thus he became early one of the "new order of men" who "came forward" and transacted the business and public work of Connecticut and the emerging nation.[33]

Other Coits served in the Continental line, Connecticut militia, and the Connecticut and Continental navies. Such was Captain William Coit, who fought at Bunker Hill and was the first commander of the armed ship *Oliver Cromwell*. Other Coits fought in the

Battle of Groton Heights or were carried away captive from New London by General Arnold after the burning of the town. Although Joshua Coit exhibited later a keen interest in military activities, it is probable that he remained a civilian because he was indispensable to the conduct of his father's mercantile business and privateering ventures. Thus he served the American cause by importing and distributing munitions and supplies and by assisting its challenge to British naval power on Long Island Sound. Nathaniel Shaw Sr., Connecticut's Naval Officer, engaged in similar mercantile business on a large scale. Joshua Coit's legal services facilitated the equipment of local privateers and the disposal of their prizes, together with those of Connecticut's armed ships and the privateers of Norwich "adventurers." He may have joined in the improvised defense of Town Hill against Arnold's regulars on the morning of September 6, 1781. He suffered moderately, his father very heavily, when Arnold destroyed New London. Their two stores, wharf, and other properties were burned along with the First Church and the business district.

Although many inhabitants left the burned town, Joshua Coit remained behind to continue his law practice and act as his father's agent. In 1782 he became clerk of the Probate Court. He was made New London's only notary public and also a justice of the peace. In this manner he became an indispensable civil functionary. His law practice revived with the maritime trade with Central America, the West Indies, and Britain after the Treaty of Paris of 1783, when British merchants resumed operations in Connecticut and the notes of the Bank of North America began to circulate.[34]

Coit became prominent in the First Ecclesiastical Society that managed the finances of the First Church. He headed the committee that collected the Society Tax on polls and taxable property in 1784. He persuaded the General Court that year to permit the renting of pews to finance repair of the temporary meeting house. He negotiated the replacement of the State Treasurer's notes owned by the Society that had been destroyed with the burning of the town. He and his father subscribed £30 in cash to finance rebuilding the First Church, for which lotteries were authorized by the General Court in 1784 and 1787. In 1788 he increased his subscription by $150 or £10/2/5 at his option.[35]

Mindful of his responsibilities as an educated gentleman, he subscribed to a share in the new library which was organized after the example of the Philogramatician Society of Lebanon. In behalf of the New London Library Company he commissioned his older brother Daniel Lathrop Coit of Norwich to lay out its fund of seven pounds two shillings for books in London, which that drug importer did in due course while abroad.[36] In public life, however, Joshua Coit was handicapped during the post-war years. Despite his successful law practice and support of Congregationalism and the library, he lacked the prestige of military or diplomatic or Congressional service in the victorious cause of American independence. Although differently composed, the Standing Order still dominated Connecticut.

CHAPTER TWO

A Novitiate in Connecticut Politics

COIT's decision to bid for eminence as a lawyer was in harmony with the new situation produced by the revolutionary movement. Before 1765 a mercantile career had been the best avenue to wealth, political leadership, and a social position. During the ensuing decade Trumbull and Hancock had seemed to symbolize the continuing importance of the merchant in American affairs. Leadership in the Revolution's civil phase passed, however, to noted attorneys such as James Otis, Patrick Henry, John Adams, Thomas Jefferson, John Dickinson, and John Jay, and in New London to Richard Law.

After the Revolution, also, Alexander Hamilton returned to New York to practice law, founded the Bank of New York, and advocated a more effective union among the states. Jay labored to transform the Confederation into an effective agency for the furtherance of American interests. Jefferson and Adams upheld these at diplomatic posts in Paris and London. These were suggestive examples for a young attorney.

The resumption of peacetime trade enhanced the profits of the bar. English exporters' agents crowded the towns, swamped the markets with English sundries, and began the collection of ante-bellum debts. However, the enforcement of Britain's trade laws curtailed American exports to Britain and British colonial markets. Large English exports to the famished American market drained it of its specie in a single year and precipitated a severe depression that continued for six years.[1] While lawyers profited from the litigation produced by this situation, their new position of public leadership imposed upon them responsibility for extricating the United States from this predicament.

Coit's contributions to the solution of the complex problems that crystallized during those critical post-war years were necessarily those of a young lawyer residing in a partially rebuilt secondary port. His calm, well-balanced temperament, which contributed largely to his success at the bar, qualified him more for behind-the-scenes influence or quiet, efficient political leadership than for a spectacular front-line oratorical role. His lack of large wealth and his inexperience restricted his political activity to Connecticut for some years.

Connecticut led during that era in the crystallization of a forward-looking policy. This resulted from the pressure of practical circumstances and the interplay between the revolutionary tradition and a surviving conservativism, which intermeshed at times with a struggle for power between rival interest groups.

The malcontents' desire to repudiate or postpone payment of the national debt laid the basis for this, but the precipitating issue in 1783 was Congress' commutation of the earlier grant of half pay to army officers for life after retirement to five full years' pay at their option. Occurring immediately before disbandment of the army, this act resulted from the northern states' protest against the earlier arrangement. They had granted additional remuneration to their Continental line officers, while the South had relied upon the Congressional grant.[2] Popular resentment at the burden imposed on taxpayers by either alternative and at the favoritism to officers in contrast to the treatment of the rank and file produced in New England a vigorous protest against commutation and precipitated attacks upon the Society of the Cincinnati, which the officers of the revolutionary army had organized.

In Connecticut, the leaders of the indifferent and Loyalist elements which had been quiescent during the Revolution emerged to arouse the populace in a vigorous anticommutarian campaign.

They persuaded the towns to send delegates to an irregular convention at Middletown. There, during four sessions that continued into 1784, they attempted to secure a revision of the Charter (the State constitution) and to overthrow the new Standing Order by electing new Assistants to the Governor's Council.[3] Thus a discredited conservativism reappeared in the then novel role of demagogue, appealing to popular discontent precipitated by the postponement of hoped-for benefits from national independence and the deepening depression. It was a formidable conservative bid for a return to power.

Simultaneously, there arose a lively literary movement, focused on Hartford and initiated during the War of Independence by young Yale College graduates. Led by Timothy Dwight, Joel Barlow, John Trumbull, and David Humphreys, it was distinguished by political satire and critical idealism. Known generally as "the Connecticut Wits," a term that stressed their literary at the expense of their substantive ideas, the group upheld the principles of the American Revolution and demanded their complete implementation in the state and nation. For a short period after 1783, the Wits made Hartford the capital of the emerging federalist mind with its important constructive potentialities.

The Wits were patronized by Colonel Jeremiah Wadsworth, whose literary interests were gradually overshadowed by preoccupation with speculation. These authors published verses and political essays, signed with pseudonyms, in the *Connecticut Courant* of Hartford and other newspapers. They frequently produced books and pamphlets. Barlow moved to Hartford in 1783 to complete his *Vision of Columbus.* There he aided Noah Webster, a Yale classmate and Litchfield law student, in securing a state copyright law. Part I of Webster's *Grammatical Institutes of the English Language,* an attempt to develop an American language, appeared that year with Barlow's encouragement. In 1784 Dr. Lemuel Hopkins moved to Hartford to join the Wits and aid Barlow and Webster in founding a literary society. They supported the abolition society, in which Dwight was also prominent. Connecticut's gradual emancipation act of that year must be attributed to the re-enforcement which the Wits brought to the antislavery cause.[4] They provided the intellectual leadership that rallied Connecticut's patriot party against the anticommutarians.

Webster was a practicing attorney in Hartford. When the anticommutarian movement was at its height in January 1784, he rode with Coit in the latter's sleigh to Norwich. In their antislavery attitudes and identification with the patriot party, if not entirely in their intellectual orientation, they had much in common. At Norwhich they conferred with Captain Joseph Coit, the Huntingtons, the Lathrops, and other prominent figures.[5]

As soon as he returned to Hartford, Webster attacked the Middletown Convention and its anticommutarian supporters in a series of contributions to the *Courant*. These were so effective that the towns recalled their delegates. In April they elected representatives and Assistants from the patriot party to the legislature. Webster's preceding appeals, "Policy of Connecticut" and "To the Members of the Convention, Whether Good or Bad," had defeated anticommutarianism while supplying the victors with a positive program. Seated more firmly in power than ever, the post-revolutionary Standing Order instituted a redress of grievances. This was combined with fostering business, strengthening Congress, and interest in substituting a federal union for the declining Confederation as Governor Jonathan Trumbull had urged in 1783.[6]

Joshua Coit's behind-the-scenes role in this development identified him firmly with the victors. They labored for the realization of an effective republicanism founded upon constitutional principles and conducted in behalf of the dominant commercial, maritime, industrial, and commercial farming elements. A suggestive parallel to Connecticut's developing polity existed in the policies pursued by the federated Dutch Republic, whose red and white striped ensign had contributed to the design of the flag of the United States.

The Connecticut followers of Noah Webster, who would soon call themselves Federalists, envisaged state and federal systems in which the interest groups identified above would enjoy government encouragement and protection. Literature would be encouraged by copyright, inventions by patents; slaves would be emancipated gradually in the states and the slave trade prohibited nationally; and the states would aid education with financial grants. This program was an expression of the emerging idea of progress which was becoming so significant a part of the American mind. At Litchfield, Oliver Wolcott Sr. accepted this conception. In imitation of Pennsylvania, he led in founding the Connecticut Agricultural Society. This stimulated agricultural improvement cooperatively, reviving and extending the fruits of Jared Eliot's pioneering work of the preceding generation under the stimulus of reviving overseas markets.

Emerging Connecticut federalism was, then, a moderate liberal movement typical of the late eighteenth century, led by educated and successful gentlemen of the new Standing Order. Its constructive implications nationally became evident to contemporaries as they were focused into the movement to strengthen the Confederation or supplant it with an effective federal union.[7] This cause was advanced inadvertently by an interstate conflict with Pennsylvania revived by the Susquehanna Company. With Barlow as secretary and allied with Ethan Allen of Vermont, this speculative enterprise reasserted its claim to the Wyoming Valley in northern Pennsylvania and precipitated a quarrel between Connecticut and Pennsylvania that Congress could not settle. Thus the alliance of the Wits with contemporary business, land speculators in this instance, exposed the ineffectiveness of the Confederation in interstate relations.[8]

Connecticut federalism, while liberal in spirit and constitutional in character, was pre-democratic, transitional between the decadent aristocratic society of Europe and the democracy of a later America. The Connecticut freemen who enjoyed the suffrage were but a small portion of the adult males. Their status rested upon property in land, upon Congregational or Episcopal church membership, and, in the case of new freemen, upon being persons of approved principles and conduct. The old established families, successful merchants, large landowners, land speculators, and prominent attorneys provided leadership in the towns. Such were the Wolcotts of Windsor and Litchfield, Colonel Wadsworth in Hartford, the Trumbulls of Lebanon, the Huntingtons and Lathrops of Norwich, the Coits of Norwich and New London, the Laws, Learneds, and Brainerds of New London. Allied with them were the Congregational clergy. Small cliques dominated the town meetings so effectively that many freemen amused themselves during the meetings with horse racing, horseshoe pitching, and tavern refreshment while the sessions arrived at preordained decisions. Hardly three thousand freemen had voted for governor in the late 1760's. Only heated contests could elicit a heavier poll during the post-Revolutionary decade. Electioneering for office was nonexistent as the politically ambitious awaited the nod of the Standing Order.

Locally and in the state government, the public service was dominated by seniority and the tradition of promoting the faithful and efficient. Hence a semipermanent but elected officialdom persisted, a continuation of the colonial tradition of self-governing Connecticut. Great prestige attached to the offices of governor, lieutenant governor, assistant, and the judgeships of the Superior Court. Former governors occupied the position of elder statesmen frequently, as was illustrated by the Wolcotts who by means of office holding, marriage, and church affiliation exercised large influence during successive generations upon political promotions and public policy. A scion of such a family—for instance the Hartford attorney Oliver Wolcott Jr., a Yale College and Litchfield Law School graduate—

could win prestige by service on the Committee of the Pay-Table at Hartford. That led subsequently to high office in the administration of President George Washington, which won him an influential position in Connecticut's Standing Order.[9]

Joshua Coit possessed the family background, personality, education, and professional standing necessary for participation and leadership in Connecticut politics. Twenty-six years of age in 1784, he was maturing as a cultivated lawyer. His powdered curled hair, gold-trimmed broadcloth coat, waistcoat, breeches, and silver-buckled shoes betokened the American gentleman. A miniature of him painted a decade later exhibits a high forehead, long, slightly beaked nose, high cheekbones, ruddy cheeks, firm mouth, and long chin dominated by kindly, wise, almost youthful eyes.[10] Handsome, skilled at the bar, and thoroughly businesslike, he practiced the gentleman's graceful art of social intercourse.

Law practice took him to Norwich and to Hartford before the Superior Court. In both towns, as in New London, he made friends. Occasionally he joined other attorneys in individual actions. In New London he joined with Richard Law in securing a writ of attachment in behalf of English merchants or other creditors. In Norwich he formed a professional liaison with young Roger Griswold, a graduate of Tapping Reeve's Litchfield Law School, who had begun a promising legal and political career in 1783. Griswold's mother was a daughter of former Governor Roger Wolcott.

In July 1789 Coit delegated to him the handling of a legal matter and certain collections at a time when the new Congress was organizing the federal government in New York under Washington's leadership:

> I'll thank you to hand the enclosed, for service—& should I not be at Norwich pray take a judgment for me—some payments are made for which they have Coit & Lathrop's Receipt:
> I was at Norwich the other day when I hoped to have closed the Ex. Jno. Temple vs. L. M. you was [*sic*] out of town & I supposed

W. M. would not do anything without Council [*sic*]—I left blank notes with Brother Thos I would send you the Ex. but for accidents that may happen had rather have the Notes sent me. I must have the [illegible] I proposed you at Court I wish the business closed —& if you trouble yourself about it would thank you to let it be done as soon as conveniently may be. I am

Your obt servt. Sin[cerely]
Joshua Coit

Roger Griswold Alderman [11]

Had Coit proposed Griswold for admission to practice before the Superior Court?

The caliber of Coit's professional standards and ethics when a third party was involved he had disclosed in August 1785 in a note to Dudley Woodbridge:

> The matter of LeRoy I dont know what has become of—at Request of M. F. Winthrop who was desired to look into the matter by Mr Le Roy I was looking it up. I found a Ballance due him from Mr. Mumford or the Sheriff (Christopher's) Estate—& deliver[ed] M. W. a statement of the matter wh he sent to L. R. this was some time since, & neither M. W. nor myself have had any further advice about the matter or authority to pursue—should it be in my power which is very uncertain I shall be very happy to serve you in getting your demand.[12]

These communications explain the growth of the Brainerd and Coit practice until it included working arrangements with attorneys in Kingston, Jamaica,[13] as well as service of a wide clientele.

As early as 1784 Coit had become a friend of Uriah Tracy, a young Litchfield attorney who had come from eastern Connecticut and upon whom the political sun would shine brightly. Mrs. Lucretia Hubbard Tracy, his mother, was Coit's cousin and shared his literary interests. His reply to her request for the loan of a book exhibited him at his witty, graceful best, equally conversant with the manuals of courtesy and the law court:

—for your very Civil & polite Billet by uncle Hubbard I feel my self obliged now to send you the 2d Vol. of Shenstone. I say nothing about it—tho' every thing I could say is rendered of no consequence by sending it—"Hail ye small sweet Courtesies of life," says [Chesterfield?] "for smooth do ye make the road of it"—he adds —"like grace and beauty which beget inclination to love at first sight" is addressing my amiable Cousin & friend Mrs. Tracy who so happily possesses the real substance of these qualities 'twould be but poor Compliment to tell her that the Resemblance of them makes me esteem her—notwithstanding the appearance of studied Compliment & flattery which to speak in law style I have in the aforewritten Instrument displayed, believe me your very sincere friend & humble servant

Joshua Coit

Mrs. L. Tracy [14]

Such qualities explained further his success at the bar, which enabled him to purchase a house, thriftily, from Amasa Learned in downtown New London on September 3, 1789.[15]

Lest it be concluded that Coit had embraced completely the speech and style of those in the larger towns who aped European aristocracy, it must be observed that he continued in command of the eastern Connecticut dialect. This he employed in conversation and correspondence later with his children, with the townsmen of New London and Norwich and the farmers of the region. His continued partnership with Brainerd, whose lack of dignity after elevation to the bench would trouble the bar, suggests a democratic aspect of Coit's social orientation that was an indubitable asset in that predominantly agricultural area. There the revolutionary radical tradition was still a force.

While recovering in property and practice from the destruction of New London, he was sent by the town as a representative to the New Haven session of the legislature in October 1784. While there he helped to consolidate the victory over the anticommutarians. Interestingly, he represented the "Lower House" repeatedly in conference committees. During their sessions Roger Sherman, the state's wisest political leader, upheld the Council's refusal to admit duty free at New London £10,000 of the merchandise of Shaler & Labor which had, allegedly erroneously, been shipped first to New York. Sherman also rejected the House's proposal to refund the duty on rum re-exported from New London to New York, which Coit had wangled as an advance toward that type of trade envisaged by the motto on New London's new seal (1784), "Mare Liberum." [16]

At that legislative session Coit joined in granting authority to Congress to levy the federal impost on certain commodities so as to liquidate the Revolutionary debt of the United States, as Congress had requested the previous year; and also in ordering payment of Connecticut's share of the interest due on the federal debt. Thus Webster's insistence in February and March that Congress' authority be made adequate to the exigencies of the Union began to bear fruit. Simultaneously, the legislature gave the state's economy a much needed stimulus. It established a system of inspection, copied from Virginia's, to standardize the quality of leading exports: beef, pork, fish, tobacco, pot and pearl ashes, and flour. It levied moderate duties on imported manufactures, improved vessel registration, and established a naval officer at Norwich.[17]

After the legislative session, Coit hurried home to New London to celebrate his last Christmas as a bachelor and to bring his courtship of young Ann Boradill Hallam to a swift climax. He had known this daughter of the successful merchant Edward Hallam since her childhood. Pretty, trained carefully in the complex duties and domestic arts of the housewife, she was well read and interested in the theater. Trained also to thrift as a merchant's daughter, she inherited her father's tenacious will, intelligence, and capacity for responsibility, which, when subsequent disaster struck her own family, would enable her to manage its affairs successfully. Coit called her Nancy, her girlhood nickname, and proposed an early marriage. In love with him, as he was with her in the restrained eastern Connecticut manner, she accepted. They were married at her home on January 2, 1785, by a visiting minister who supplied the pulpit of the First Church. They then established themselves in a modest house situated a few blocks from The Parade.[18]

In April, Coit was sent again to the legislature as a representative of New London, together with Major William Hillhouse. They traveled this time to Hartford, the other state capital, for the annual Election Day and ensuing session. Coit was placed at once on the Committee of Assistants and Representatives, headed by Roger Sherman, which counted the freemen's ballots. Sherman then reported the election of Matthew Griswold, Governor, and Samuel Huntington of Norwich, Lieutenant Governor, and the election of Coit's colleague, Hillhouse, to the Council as an Assistant.[19]

During the four weeks that followed, Coit completed his novitiate as a legislator. Legislation was, however, only part of the work of the "Lower House." It joined the Council in appointing the judges of the Superior, county, probate, and justice courts; the officers of the militia; the surveyors of lands; and the naval officers. In other words, the legislature controlled the state patronage. Participation in this annual distribution of the offices enhanced Coit's political influence in New London, which with Middletown and Hartford had been chartered as a city the year before. Hence, he was credited locally with some responsibility for the appointment of Hillhouse as judge of the New London County Court, and of Gurdon Saltonstall as judge of the County Probate Court. Coit, with his relative Benjamin Coit, was continued among the sixty-three justices of the peace of New London County.[20]

During that May and June, the legislature renewed the impost and excise laws that serviced the state debt and financed a part of current expenses. Although the continued tax abatement to New London "sufferers" from Arnold's raid (including Coit and his father) was of only local importance, the act taxing shipping for the repair and maintenance of the New London lighthouse was important to the economy of the entire state.

Merchants and lawyers were gratified by the act for the collection of book debts. The legal profession welcomed the improvised procedure provided by the Act for the Settlement of Testate and Intestate Estates and other improvements in the courts. Rum manufacturers were pleased with the continued duty on imported rum. Noah Webster's followers were gratified by the authorization granted to Congress to prohibit trade with nations with which the United States had no commercial treaties and also by the power delegated to Congress to regulate commerce for fifteen years if nine states concurred. This was vigorous support for John Jay's attempts to negotiate commercial treaties with Great Britain and Spain in behalf of the Confederation. Coit's role in the enactment of these portions of the Connecticut Federalists' program, as Webster's friend and as the champion of New London and commercial and legal interests, was not without significance.[21]

Midway during the session Jedediah Strong of Litchfield, Clerk of the House of Representatives, returned home. Coit, to his surprise, was elected Clerk in his stead. This was an unusual responsibility for a delegate attending his second session. His interest in the improvement of the courts, expressed in a letter to his law partner, and in the appointments and pending legislation, hardly explains this preferment. That must be attributed to his association with Webster in the defeat of the anticommutarians and the subsequent enactment of the Federalist legislative program.

A year earlier, as a part of it, the legislature had voted that the judges of the Superior Court should hold office "during the pleasure of the assembly." This gratification of the property interests' desire for indefinite judicial tenure similar to Great Britain's was an early expression of the sentiment that would produce life tenure for federal judges three years later in the federal Constitution. The novelty of this earlier provision was such that in Connecticut it precipitated a hostile reaction, which led during the spring of 1785 to the repeal of the judicial act of 1784, despite Coit's support of the strong minority that desired its continuance.[22] Thus the legislature returned to the earlier practice of annual election of the judges.

Coit was as yet a tertiary political figure. Hillhouse and Law of New London and Benjamin Huntington of Norwich sat in the Council with Samuel Huntington. As Assistants, they belonged to the Standing Order.[23] Obviously, the political importance of the two towns transcended that of their population. New London's was approximately five thousand, but its property valuation had not equaled Norwich's or New Haven's since before Arnold's raid.

Coit's term of service as substitute Clerk was an indication of his prospects. However, he was not re-elected to that office at the October session at New Haven. This he attended with Amasa Learned, Yale College 1772, a former teacher in the Union School of New London, licensed preacher, recently the New London lighthouse keeper, and also intermarried with the Hallams. It remained to be seen which of these two New London representatives would ascend the political ladder more rapidly.

Together they supported New Haven's incorporation as a city. They gave earnest attention to the improvement of stage roads, regulation of ferries, and the confused state of the currency. Of the latter nine types were in circulation, only one of which was coin. The others were: Continental bills, orders on the Civil List, soldiers' notes, interest certificates on moneys loaned "to this State," Connecticut "Bills," orders on receipts of specific taxes, "Morris Notes," and "Inlay's Certificates." This situation made thoroughly explicable the interest of Coit and other associates of Noah Webster in the organization of a more effective federal government.[24] A national currency would be among its earliest achievements. Coit was on special guard against paper-money proposals that October,[25] a year before the paper-money craze in other states would alarm com-

JOSHUA COIT
By James Peale, 1794
Courtesy of Robert S. Coit

mercial and large landed interests and give impetus to the demand for an effective union.

Thus, while the Connecticut delegates in Congress waged a long campaign beside other northern men to secure to the Confederation adequate revenue and commercial powers and to open foreign markets that would alleviate the post-war depression, Coit's political activity contributed to consolidation of the patriot—now Federalist—party's dominance in Connecticut by stimulating commerce and industry and attempting to increase Congress' authority in key areas.

Although he submitted a large tax "list" for New London annually and enjoyed a successful practice, Coit's inconsiderable fortune would have prevented him from serving in the Congress of the Confederation or the federal Congress of 1789 had he been elected to either. Meanwhile, he added to his law library. As early as October 1785 he had purchased "an Irish set of Burrow's Reports" with other professional books from New York City, a significant indication of his interest in British law and precedent.[26]

As Clerk of the House during the previous spring he had signed all enacted bills, and approved petitions and commissions of appointment. He was undoubtedly proud of his signature on the act regularizing and extending the benefits of the Toleration Act of 1784 beyond the Baptists to other specified non-Congregational religious associations. Such further modification of the century-old religious monopoly that his own denomination had enjoyed was in harmony with the religious liberalism that he and other Congregationalists in the legislature shared.[27] Like deism, toleration was an ingredient of the federal liberalism of the new Standing Order, whose trans-Atlantic counterpart might have been discovered among the "enlightened" Whig aristocracy of Great Britain.

CHAPTER THREE

From Legislature to Congress

C oit's rapport with the Hartford bar and literary community was strengthened on October 14, 1786, when Noah Webster arrived by vessel from Providence on a lecture tour in behalf of an American language. After depositing his bags at "Mr. Miner's" inn he waited "on Mr J Coit." The next day he attended service at the First Church: "Heard Mr. Channing. Dine at Mr Dudley Salton- stall P M at Church hear the Bishop [Samuel Seabury]. Drink tea with Mr Richard. Intro'd to Mr Winthrop & family Peggy is very handsome," noted the susceptible bachelor in his diary. On Tuesday he lectured to a slender audience of fourteen. Then he supped "with Mr. Coit." The following day he read books by the notable pro- American English liberal philosophers, "Priestley [1] & Price," [2] loaned to him by a Mr. Rose. Their circulation in New London attested to an "enlightened" interest in science, philosophy, and radical thought that confirmed the revolutionary heritage and prepared for an in- tense interest in and sympathy for the first stage of the French Rev- olution. After that Webster departed for Norwich, where he lec- tured twice, "to 24" and then "to a handsome audience." [3]

Coit returned to the legislature in May 1787. He was again elected Clerk of the "Lower House." [4] Almost four months after its adjournment, he and his wife presented their first-born, Robert, to the First Church for baptism when he was nearly two years old. The baptism on September 23 strengthened their relationship with that influential congregation immediately after adjournment of the Federal Convention at Philadelphia.[5] Coit did not attend the Octo- ber legislative session, nor did he in January 1788 attend the state convention which ratified the federal Constitution. To that, Richard Law and Amasa Learned were the New London delegates.

On Election Day in May, however, Coit was again in the "Lower House," and a member of the joint legislative Election Committee. But Learned replaced him in the October and January sessions at New Haven, the latter of which reported the freemen's Congressional nominees.[6] In May 1789 Coit was back in the House of Representatives at Hartford. He served there with the abolitionist Zephaniah Swift as one of the two Clerks of the House. Among the papers that Coit signed was a resolution authorizing buoys on the reefs and rocks at the mouth of New London harbor, in which he was much interested, and the act appointing a state commissioner to negotiate with the Indians of the Western Reserve. This was the area Congress had granted Connecticut on the south shore of Lake Erie in northeast Ohio in lieu of its sea-to-sea charter claim.[7]

In May 1792 he was again in the legislature, serving on the Election Committee and as a Clerk of the House. His influential position enabled him quietly to secure the enactment of several measures vitally important to New London that were also profitable to him. Two years previously he had signed a long petition requesting a lottery to finance repair of the post road through the Mohegan Indian lands between New London and Norwich. Now, since those repairs had depreciated, he secured legislative approval of another petition. This established Connecticut's first turnpike on that highway, whose tolls were to finance its regular maintenance. Of this turnpike Coit was appointed a commissioner.[8]

A fortnight later he informed Brainerd, his law partner, that although "little extraordinary" legislation was pending, he anticipated favorable action upon a New London and Norwich petition for chartering a bank at New London of the type that Noah Webster had advocated in the *Connecticut Courant*. In the previous August Coit had written to his brother Daniel at Norwich of the prospects of the Bank of the United States and of "the fashion of banking." Next to the Lathrops of Norwich, the Coits were the largest subscribers to the new bank's stock. Joshua Coit had figured in the bank's preliminary organization, which had begun business before application for a charter. His influence, coupled with that of the promoters of a Hartford bank, secured charters for both from a legislature anxious to stimulate the entire economy. Thus he aided Webster's, Colonel Wadsworth's, and Alexander Hamilton's attempt to elevate the United States from a semibarter to a mercantile-money economy.

Simultaneously, Webster assisted Coit also "in copying the bill" to grant five hundred thousand acres of the Western Reserve to "the sufferers" from British incursions during the Revolution. As a "sufferer" personally and via his father's losses, Joshua Coit received a portion of these lands. Probably he sold them to his brother Daniel Lathrop Coit, the Norwich drug importer and a director of the new Union Bank of New London. For years afterward Daniel L. Coit would attempt to market those lands, agitating for a canal to Lake Erie from the Hudson River so as to make them accessible and provide them with a transportation outlet to markets.

Joshua Coit's report to Brainerd expressed, significantly, an interest in the freemen's spring nominations for Congress.[9] Probably respect for the proprieties led him on the second Thursday of May to ask the senior Clerk, Uriah Tracy, to sign the Union Bank's charter in his stead. Coit had invested in it. Like Hamilton, he had secured the charter incidentally for his own enrichment while furthering the interests of the mercantile community that the new bank would serve. He believed sincerely in its efficacy,[10] and he was vindicated by the stimulus that it gave to the economic development of the Thames River valley. General Jedediah Huntington, Collector of the Port at New London and formerly on Washington's staff, became the Union Bank's first president. John Hallam, Joshua Coit's brother-in-law, was elected the first cashier. Joshua Coit was elected a director in 1793. He added to his stockholding steadily until he became one of the largest investors in the bank. So closely was he identified with the interests of the New London and Norwich mercantile communities that it was believed that he could not be interested in service in Congress.

Thus Coit became a typical northern Federalist statesman actively engaged in fostering commerce and banking. Unlike Colonel Wadsworth or Amasa Learned, who had gone to Congress in 1789 and 1791 respectively, Coit did not speculate in depreciated United States war bonds or in western lands. More cautious, he preferred investment in the Union Bank. As the gradual inflation of values that characterized the early Federalist period began, it was evident that he had achieved moderate affluence and a position of considerable political influence.

In May 1793, after the fall of the French monarchy and the outbreak of war between Britain and France, he became senior Clerk of the House of Representatives at Hartford at the head of a staff of three, including Swift. Uriah Tracy was elected Speaker, confirming eastern Connecticut's and Litchfield's influence in the House.[11] The session was notable in Coit's private life because of the receipt there of his first letter from his six-year-old son Robert.

His reply was phrased in his section's variation of the American English.

Well Bob, you are a good Boy for writing me by your uncle Leverett, but you gave me a mighty short letter;—your Journal & the Garden I want much to hear how they come on—have you had any Rain since I have gone? and how do you contrive to set your self to work now you have no School?—I am afraid you lay a bed too late these warm mornings. I want you to be up by sunrise & a playing about before Breakfast—this will make you grow strong & hearty; I wonder if Mr Gorden has sowed that hayseed in the Lot —he promised to do it before I came away, & I am very sorry he did not, for I want to have it growing—do you try to find him & get him to do it. I'm glad to hear that Fanny runs about. you tell her there is a little girl here not above half so big as she is & I have not heard her cry but once since I have been at Hartford. I wish Lydia—you may not have cryed [*sic*] but once apiece since I cam [*sic*] from home. you must write in your Mama's next letter a good long one—give my love to all the children, Aunt Leveret & Grandma.

I am your loving father
Joshua Coit

Mr. Robert Coit [12]

By this time Coit was being considered seriously for Congress. In Connecticut at that time each Congressman represented the entire state. Election was proof, therefore, of having achieved state-wide influence, of enjoying the approval of the Standing Order, and of having been admitted into its outer circle. The inclusion of nominations for Congressmen in the freemen's primary every biennium, and occasional voting on the Congressional and state nominees together in April, assimilated the federal elections to the Connecticut system. The Federalists were as yet its only political party. At times an important figure was nominated, even elected, as Assistant and Congressman simultaneously, or would resign from Congress to accept a judgeship on the Superior Court. For some years to come the office of Governor outranked that of United States Senator in prestige, probably because the former not only headed the administration but also presided at the Council and over the Supreme Court of Errors, which had been created in 1784.[13]

During the summer of 1793 the position of Congressmen came to be recognized as one of growing importance but one involving considerable personal hazard. The Caribbean yellow fever struck Philadelphia, the national capital, in a terrible epidemic. The high mortality and the disease's inexplicable character precipitated a mass flight from the city to the interior, and intensified medical attempts to ascertain the cause and perfect a remedy more effective than Dr. Benjamin Rush's intensive bleeding of the stricken.[14]

To make matters worse for Washington's administration and its supporters, Citizen Genêt, the newly arrived Minister of the new French Republic, had flouted national authority. He had commissioned privateers after landing at Charleston, South Carolina, and during a leisurely journey of two months to Philadelphia had conspired with George Rogers Clark for the invasion of Spanish Louisiana. There, after a proconsul's welcome, Genêt had cultivated the new Democratic-Republican Clubs in an open attempt to organize French political influence via Thomas Jefferson's new Republican Party. This activity aggravated the danger, which Washington had attempted to forestall before Genêt's arrival at the capital by a proclamation of neutrality, that the unarmed United States would be drawn into the War of the French Revolution on the side of France. The Franco-American treaty of alliance of 1778 asserted the principle of "free ships make free goods," the code of Europe's small-navy powers, in opposition to the British practice, and also obligated the United States to protect the French West Indies. While influential Federalists such as Benjamin Goodhue of Salem, Massachusetts, labored to prevent American involvement in the war, Genêt ignored the proclamation of neutrality. With enthusiastic popular approval, he demanded full observation of the treaty of alliance while flouting the proclamation of neutrality by licensing an American privateer at Philadelphia. Thus he challenged the authority and dignity of the federal government.

Open to invasion by land and sea, the United States was virtually defenseless. It was dependent upon British finance and, following the outbreak of the war, upon British markets to an unusual degree. Yet the federal government was confronted by powerful popular sympathy for the harassed, invaded French Republic and its professed principles. Such sympathy was especially strong in New London. It threatened to force an ill-considered intervention in the war, due in part to gratitude for French aid during the War of Independence, which Genêt and the Clubs fostered sedulously.

Americans were pleased that their new sister republic seemed to be patterning its constitutional system after that of the United States. They were thrilled at the "flattering" prospect "that the tyrannical rule of despots" in Europe "is to be corrected." They were susceptible to the appeal that they should repay France's decisive intervention of 1778 in the American Revolution with a similar action in its behalf.

Connecticut Federalists were outraged by Genêt's improper and "insulting" conduct toward the federal government. Of this they were informed by Oliver Wolcott Jr., Comptroller of the Treasury of the United States, in his correspondence with his relatives and Noah Webster. Wolcott reminded Webster, for example, of the tragic experiences of ancient Greece and Rome and of modern Sweden and Poland that had resulted from foreign interventions.[15] Nevertheless, the *Connecticut Courant* and the (New London) *Connecticut Gazette* filled their columns with the latest news of France's defense, evincing a more strong than cautious friendship for that nation among the freemen and the unenfranchised masses. The *Gazette* had published earlier and serially Part I of Thomas Paine's *The Rights of Man,* illustrating again the greater liberalism of the New London area. That dated from the organization there of the first Sons of Liberty in Connecticut.[16] However, the Federalists there and elsewhere became apprehensive that the Clubs organized in imitation of the Jacobin Society might precipitate a "democratic revolution" and "reign of terror" such as had occurred in France.

Thus the mildly liberal, elitist, newly established Federalist regime, including Washington's administration and Connecticut's Standing Order, was confronted suddenly with the specter of a dynamic, foreign-inspired, revolutionary extension of the principles upon which it was founded before it had consolidated its ascendancy in the United States.

There was implicit in this an unrecognized danger that the Republicans' and Clubs' appeals to the crowd, plus the dangerous international situation, might precipitate the ruling Federalists into an emotional, blind defense of their "untitled republican aristocracy" that would stultify their liberal principles. The open avowal by Fisher Ames of the Massachusetts Essex Junto (after John Adams' example of 1788) of his conviction that only "the wise, the rich, and the good" were fit to rule, with reference to British Toryism,[17] although provoked by the cry of *"ça ira"* in American streets, defined what became an inescapable political issue as the Connecticut legislature convened in New Haven in October. Aristocracy when it ceased to be liberal and progressive was no longer defensible in America, however.

Washington's formal demand for Genêt's recall, after the latter's June appeal over his head to the public to force America's entry into the war as France's ally, had vindicated American sovereignty and preserved neutrality. Many Federalists, however, continued to be friendly to France and interested in its new doctrines. Such were Vice President John Adams and Ezra Stiles.[18]

The tense international and domestic political situations demanded Congressmen of greater acumen and self-restraint. The Wolcott leadership in Connecticut, therefore, quietly arranged for the elevation to Congress of younger men of this type to fill two vacancies in the state's delegation. The Wolcotts also pushed others for nomination for Assistants.

When the legislature convened for its October session in New Haven, Coit was promptly elected Speaker of the House of Representatives. Then the report of the Elections Committee disclosed that he ranked fifteenth among twenty nominees for the twelve Assistants in the Council. Two of them were ex officio Assistants, Governor Huntington and Lieutenant Governor Oliver Wolcott Sr. The other ten were those who ranked highest in freemen's votes received. This excluded Coit from the "upper house." Below him in votes received for Assistants were his friends Griswold, Swift, Colonel Wadsworth, and Chauncey Goodrich, a Hartford attorney who had worked with Webster in the chartering of the Hartford Bank in 1792. Goodrich would soon be Wolcott Jr.'s brother-in-law.[19]

This was preliminary to filling the vacancies in the Congressional delegation that had been held over since May, when the press had opposed the selection of Tapping Reeve and Swift. They had become next in line because of the withdrawal of higher ranking nominees for Congress to accept legislative appointment to the Superior Court. Swift had been denounced then as "only a lukewarm Federalist."

Accordingly, the legislature presented to the freemen on November 11 the names of Coit, Swift, Griswold, James Davenport, Goodrich, Nathaniel Smith, and Samuel Whittlesey Dana. Goodrich headed the committee canvassing the returns and announced the election of Coit and Swift on December 2. The former's poll of 2189 freemen's votes in the special town meetings was far in advance of Swift's 1663. The defeated nominees were sent to Congress subsequently as future vacancies occurred.[20]

The Federalist leaders and freemen wanted Coit to be in Congress during the crucial months ahead, although there was doubt that he would accept. He did so, yielding to quiet pressure despite his wife's opposition, an attitude to which she adhered for months after the yellow fever epidemic subsided and he had begun his service in Philadelphia. The citizens had returned to that city and resumed their normal activities when he and Swift arrived after a hurried journey, two weeks after the Third Congress began its long session.

In reply to Mrs. Coit's misgivings lest "political pursuits engage my attention more than Family & home," Coit admitted to her that assuming his seat in Congress was "a kind of political lottery." Obviously, he hoped that it would lead to higher office, very probably in Connecticut. "It will be for the best," he predicted. He wrote to her regularly before every post and to Robert as well, continuing *in absentia* his guidance of their home and children's training.[21] Possibly he regretted not having waited to come to Philadelphia until he had presided at Hartford as Speaker of the House in the spring. His membership in Congress necessitated withdrawing also from the directorate of the Union Bank.

Unlike Swift, who participated actively in the debates, Coit made no recorded speeches and only occasionally moved the previous question during that Congressional session. Undoubtedly he was briefed by Amasa Learned and Uriah Tracy, who were farther along in their first terms. Coit agreed with the latter that it was unwise to "make laws by the rod" lest "mischief" accrue. He avoided land speculation, in which Learned had invested his funds. Perhaps it was at this time that Coit purchased a share in the Bank of the United States, thus identifying himself with Hamilton's financial system.[22]

His first vote opposed attaching an appropriation to the authorization to employ the navy against the "Algerines." His second vote was also in the minority, in opposition to recommitting a Senate bill to alter the flag of the United States slightly. Then he joined the majority in rejecting half pay for life for army officers serving three years or more, an action in harmony with Connecticut sentiment. In this manner he established his reputation for independent judgment and voting consistent with the tradition established by the "country" members of the British Parliament during the seventeenth century. Many Federalist Congressmen and Senators avowed fidelity to this practice despite their vigorous support of Hamilton's policy.

Comprehension of the character and function of political parties was as yet imperfect. This was attributable to recent association of the Loyalists with disloyalty during the War of Independence and currently to French intrigues with the Republican Party. The role of the independent gentleman Congressman Coit would essay again toward the close of his career during an era of rapidly rising partisanship as national political parties developed their unique function. His family background, Harvard College education, and experience in the burning of New London prevented him from becoming an Anglophile. This differentiated him from the more ardent Hamiltonians.

He became the second man on the select committee that received numerous petitions for protective duties on imports competing with American manufactures. He voted for the Eleventh Amendment to the Constitution. He stood with the Connecticut delegation and the Essex Junto in voting to authorize construction of four heavy frigates to protect American shipping from the Algerines and from harm during the European war. Although at first Coit regarded the beginning of "a Naval Establishment" as a necessary "Evil," before long he was asking "without a fleet the question occurs where is the security" of American trade and coasts? This navy bill was an oblique reply to the hotly resented British seizures of some three hundred American vessels in the West Indies under new Orders in Council. Those seizures had precipitated a sudden crisis in Anglo-American relations soon after Genêt's recall to France.[23] Many anticipated an Anglo-American war because of the recent incendiary speech to the Indians by Governor General Lord Dorchester of Canada. That had inflamed the American West.

In this emotionally charged situation Coit calmly secured an act providing buoys at the entrance to New London harbor and in Providence River, Rhode Island, in behalf of the maritime trade.

In the Southern states anti-British feeling was intensified by British creditors' continued attempts to collect pre-Revolutionary plantation debts and by hostility to the revived British commercial monopoly of the staple trade. This attitude the Republicans appealed to in an outcry against the Orders in Council, British intrigues with the Indians of the Northwest, vessel seizures in the West Indies that even Hamilton called "atrocious," and impressment of American sailors. These issues enabled Jefferson's party to recruit a popular following in Northern cities also. Simultaneously, the injuries inflicted upon their constituents obliged some Northern Federalists to support strong measures to force Great Britain to negotiate a treaty of commerce, which their party and region had long desired.

A huge majority in Congress imposed a thirty-day embargo in retaliation for seizures of American vessels in the West Indies by Britain and France, despite the six-weeks' opposition to this measure of a determined minority including Coit. Then a general boycott of Great Britain was proposed. That alarmed Coit, who feared that such a measure would precipitate hostilities with Great Britain. Because of the vulnerability of the Hamiltonian financial system, which rested upon import duties, and because of the extreme differences between North and South, he opposed involvement in the European war lest such a course lead to destruction of the national government. To forestall the boycott, Washington sent John Jay as special envoy to London to negotiate a general settlement of differences. Coit was much gratified. He had concluded that negotiation with Great Britain had become the only alternative to war. Simultaneously, the President dispatched General "Mad Anthony" Wayne to the Northwest Territory to deal with the Indians. The Republicans then talked of sequestering British debts in retaliation for the vessel seizures and denounced Jay as biased against the South and incompetent. The Clubs opposed any negotiation with "our antient enemy." [24] Coit regarded with amazement a so-called citizens' meeting in the State House yard, where neither debate nor dissent was permitted.

The sectional feeling engendered between Northern and Southern men in Congress during this crisis became intense. It revived in the mind of Senator Rufus King of New York, Hamilton's representative, a strongly held conviction of 1785-1786 that the opposing sections were so dissimilar in interests that their effective union was impossible. Learning that Virginia's Senator John Taylor of Caroline was about to leave Congress, King proposed seriously to him in a committee room early in May, in the presence and with the approval of Senator Oliver Ellsworth of Connecticut, that amicable separation of North and South be accomplished by "a friendly intercourse among the members" of Congress. At this time Jay was waiting to sail from New York. (A year previously Wolcott Jr. had intimated that disunion might result from sectional incompatibility arising from the burden of Southern plantation debts. Such a division of the Union, he had asserted to his father, should be friendly but "eternal.")

Taylor rejected King's proposal. He informed Madison of it confidentially. That word of King's attempt, provoked by the Republicans' bitter opposition to Jay's mission and an accommodation with Great Britain, circulated in Congressional committee rooms may be conjectured.[25] At least two Northern Senators, speaking possibly for a larger number of Federalists, preferred to jettison the South and negotiate an arrangement between the commercial North and Great Britain.

Coit also had noted how antipathy to Hamilton's funding system and the Bank of the United States, together with hatred of Great Britain, had motivated the Southern members' "French frenzy" and proposal of non-importation of British manufactures. During the hottest debates he had feared that differences between North and South over the Hamiltonian financial system and commercial policy, plus a variance of views toward French democracy, threatened the existence of the Union, particularly if the United States became involved in the War of the French Revolution. By late April, however, he was not so sure that the progress of time might not assimilate North and South and that "dissolution ought not to be apprehended from that quarter." From this conclusion he apparently did not deviate in future years.

Coit, with Learned, James Hillhouse, and the other Connecticut Congressmen, supported the Administration staunchly during the prolonged struggle to prevent the crisis from precipitating war. As an experienced politician, Coit kept a weather eye on public opinion. Its "passions," he observed to his wife in late March, "seem every day to grow warmer on the subject, and this indicates no favourable Event." Conceding that it "is fashionable to be angry at the British," he continued:

> Indeed we have but too much cause. Old animosities are revived by recent injuries, and our attachment to the French is in degree increased in proportion to the British animosity. Fortunately perhaps, we have but too much cause to complain of the French. A Large number of our vessells are detained & have been for a long time since in their Ports. I say fortunately for if the ill usage we have received was all from one side there would be more danger of our entering into the War; 'tis of infinite Consequence I believe that we keep out of it. I believe we may, but if oppressed much more our passions I fear will get the better of our Prudence & then everything must be put to the hazard.

To this frank statement he added that perhaps it was "my wishes rather than my judgment which lead me to think more favourably than others of Peace and War. 'Tis in fact a Business of much uncertainty." While hoping for "a peace this Summer," he remarked to Mrs. Coit that they then could consider at leisure his proposal that they remove from New London to the farm he proposed to buy in Montville up the Thames River.[26] There his family would be safe from British naval raids should the worst occur.

Although this letter's contents may have been somewhat reassuring to his New London friends, on April 10 a young friend and attorney of that city, Elias Perkins, who was also interested in the Union Bank, wrote Coit of his desire for continued peace with Europe. Coit replied bluntly but cogently to that former law student of Senator Ellsworth's, asking "what are the means most probable to secure it, & is peace compatible with national honour & Security of our property?" Jay's appointment seemed "much disliked by our Southern Folks" as being hostile to their legislative demands. "Antient party Combinations" prejudiced proceedings. One element wished "to negotiate & prepare for the worst, but to take no Step that will hazard the *little* or the *much* you have to hope from negotiations." The opposition was urging insincerely "that Sequestration of British Debts & suspension of importations of British Manufactures will give weight to Negotiations" whose failure they seemed to desire.

He rejected the Southern assertion that the Connecticut delegation did not reflect the views of its constituents on these questions. Although, he remarked to Perkins, he would "not be surprised if men of warm feeling resenting the Injuries which America has suffered from G Britain should pretty readily advocate those measures which have been proposed by the Southern people," not five of the next most likely hundred men in Connecticut who could be selected to replace the present delegation would "have voted differently from their present Representatives. Tell me what you think of my calculations." [27]

Although the Connecticut members vainly opposed a month's extension of the embargo, they rallied sufficient support after four more weeks of acrimony to defeat the boycott bill and avoid war, which might well have resulted from such retaliation for British seizures and impressments.[28] Thus they successfully supported the policy of non-involvement in European wars which Wolcott Jr. had outlined previously to Noah Webster, now editor of the *American Minerva* in New York City.

In early May 1794 Wolcott Jr. warned Webster also that French principles were incompatible with "existing society." The "American citizen's" duty in "this interesting period . . . is obvious, we ought carefully to guard against any deterioration in our principles —to resist all novelties and innovations, to respect ourselves, to of-

fend none, to be prepared for defence against invasions & intrigues
—and above all, to come to an absolute determination that we will
on no account become a party to the War." [29] The Comptroller of
the Treasury wrote his father, the Lieutenant Governor, on that
same day that "the fortunes of America and the destiny of republicanism, depend on the stability of the northern States. . . . Our
people here [Philadelphia] and to the southward, are much cheated
by their false professions and their intrigues, and there is real danger of some violent explosion." [30]

This defined, undoubtedly after discussions with Hamilton but
lacking that Secretary's interregionalism, the creed which the Yale-
Litchfield men and the Wits of Connecticut would uphold during
the first of the ensuing years of crisis. Its vigorous Americanism and
confidence in the New England way, linked as they were with Gallophobia and anti-Southernism, rested upon a new conservativism.
This repudiated for the duration of the crisis the idea of "improvement" that had distinguished Connecticut federalism before the ad-
vent of Washington's administration. But its Americanism appeared
to limit loyalty to that mode of life existent in the region north of
the Delaware River or to that east of the Hudson. The danger implicit in such a position, when King's and Ellsworth's proposals to
John Taylor of a week later are kept in view, is obvious. Did these
statements provide the rationale also of that attempt to arrange a
peaceful division of the Union in behalf of shortsighted Northern
interests? Why, the perceptive reader will ask, did the formulation
of this conservative Northern credo synchronize with the launching
of Jay's mission and the King-Ellsworth abortive coup?

Although Coit loyally supported the Administration policy of
non-involvement and emergency negotiation, he was not called
upon immediately to accept this new conservativism or to react to
the revival of Northern separatism. Eventually, when Governor
Wolcott Sr. subscribed to his son's creed and provisionally to its

logic of interregional relations, Coit would be confronted with a test of his political loyalty to the Wolcott faction which was upholding a regional policy at variance with his views.

For the present, he was interested in the implications of the popular turbulence whipped up by the Democratic Club in Philadelphia and of the acrimonious, partisan Congressional debate before Britain's modification of the Orders in Council deflated the war spirit. On the last day of March he had observed calmly to his wife, as if in validation of the Hamiltonian view of human motivation, "Great Bodies of Men move more as Passions & Incidents of the moment direct. Fortunately their Numbers generally prevent them from moving very fast. New incidents arise and time is given to grow cool & reflect." Obviously, Coit had become involved as a new member in the deepening party cleavage as the result of his firm support of the Administration.[31]

In May he voted together with Fisher Ames, his Harvard friend and eloquent spokesman of the Essex Junto, to impose a stamp tax instead of a lawyers' license tax to raise new revenue, and to admit to American ports prizes taken from nations with whom the United States was at peace! Yet he voted with the moderate Federalists and Republicans in defeating an increase in the army which Hamilton desired. However, Coit and Learned vainly supported a bill to raise a regiment for the defense of the southwestern frontier, which would have accomplished this on a limited scale to meet an immediate, domestic need. Evidently both men were actuated by no such circumscribed provincialism as was burgeoning among the Wolcotts and their following. Instead, they followed Hamilton in supporting an intersectional polity that would strengthen the position of the Federalists in the South.[32]

Although this course may not have won the full approval of the Comptroller of the Treasury, it satisfied Coit's seniors in Congress and the Connecticut freemen to such an extent that the latter nominated Coit fourth on the list of fourteen Congressional candidates with a poll close to Jonathan Trumbull Jr.'s at the head of the list, and six hundred votes higher than Griswold's and Swift's. Then, in October 1794, the freemen elected Coit fourth in the new Congressional delegation behind Trumbull Jr., Hillhouse, and Tracy. In this manner he won his way into the middle group of Federalist leaders of Connecticut.[33]

CHAPTER FOUR

A Liberal Federalist at Washington's Court

COIT's success despite the fact that he did not make a formal speech in the Third Congress during 1793–1794 was attributable to several factors. His Harvard College background made him acceptable to the Massachusetts Federalists such as Fisher Ames, who had preceded him as a leader of the Speaking Club. Coit's identification with banking and commerce ensured his compatibility with the Hamiltonians. His intellectual interests made him agreeable to Federalists of more liberal views. Furthermore, he was socially acceptable in Washington's capital, where the character and manners of a gentleman were as essential as political orthodoxy.

This brilliant but partial reproduction of European court and metropolitan society shone more brightly than ever between Christmas 1793 and the summer of 1794. Mrs. Coit's decision to remain in New London with their small children diminished Joshua Coit's zest for Philadelphia society. She was the more sociable. When not at committee meetings, he spent many evenings with his books and correspondence. Yet, as his letters to "Dr. Nancy" and "Bob" disclose, he participated in the Washingtons' formal court. He attended the theater and occasional balls. His education, Congressional friendships, and intimacy with Noah Webster assured him as much social recognition as he desired.

From his brother Daniel, who had enjoyed the friendship of Benjamin Franklin and the Marquis de Lafayette in Paris, he had learned of European court life.[1] Hence Joshua Coit exhibited no flattered gratification when he was invited to the President's weekly dinners for Congressmen. The sociability and excellent and exotic food, together with the style set by the expensive porcelain on the long table, facilitated Washington's leadership. These dinners also assisted him in creating a spirit of fellowship among the Federalist and, as they appeared, Republican Congressmen.

Each week also the President held a levee, at which officialdom, Senators, Congressmen, merchants, landowners, and attorneys presented themselves, bowed, were received with a bow, and then mingled with each other informally, wearing the accepted dress of gentlemen. Lacking titles, termed "Excellency" only if of high official station, those present were predominantly Federalist. Analogous to the levees of the British and French courts, these events contributed significantly to the establishment at the capital of the "Republican Court," which visiting European aristocrats found congenial. Attendance there and the Washingtons' approval were essential to full acceptance in the socio-political circle of Federalism.[2]

At these gatherings, and at Mrs. Washington's weekly levees also, the cultivated, astute Oliver Wolcott Jr. circulated, observed, and advised the Connecticut men while helping to strengthen the New England influence. His intimacy with Senator George Cabot, Fisher Ames, aand Stephen Higginson explains the rapport that persisted for years in Congress between the Connecticut and Massachusetts Federalists. While briefing Noah Webster on policy problems, he encouraged him to write a history of New England that would stress New England "manners, customs and institutions" and the "guaranty for republican systems" provided by "civil and religious corporations" and thereby prevent "the people from adopting any novelties in this age of theory and nonsense." He was, he admitted, "an enthusiast, if not a fanatic, with respect to the customs of the northern States."[3]

The Federalist gentry generally became more articulately conservative as the Clubs staged mass demonstrations in behalf of the French Republic and in opposition to Washington's neutrality. Yet early in 1794 Congress adjourned as a body and joined the

Philadelphia Democratic Club in a tremendous, excited celebration of the French defeat of the Duke of York's invading army. This was duplicated in New London with day-long bell ringing, religious services, and general tribute to the "Rights of Man," universal liberty, and the brotherhood of man.[4] Nevertheless, their reaction to the French Revolution and the Clubs gradually de-emphasized the Federalists' liberal orientation which, in Connecticut, had led Timothy Dwight to admit girls to his Greenfield Hill Academy.[5]

Yet, despite the fact that as early as December 1792 Wolcott Jr. had rejected the "strange kind of reasoning" which supposed "that the liberties of America depend on the right of cutting throats in France," the United States Mint placed on its first ten-dollar gold piece the head of Liberty wearing the Roman Liberty Cap after the fashion revived by the American revolutionaries and French Jacobin sans-culottes. Vice President John Adams continued to cultivate Physiocratic economic theory, which was at variance with Hamilton's commercial banking and fiscal system.[6] However, among all members of the Federalist Party the conviction that the Constitution and its supporting political theory were original and successful products of the application of reason to political organization and leadership in a manner that effectively restrained popular "passions" tended to insulate them from the influence of French republicanism which a large part of the American masses found so captivating.

During 1793–1797 Washington's court was a means of rallying the Federalists to oppose French intrigues and "democratic" coups in the United States. This "Lady" Washington made evident by her indignant association of bad manners and dress with "filthy democrats." Her example encouraged Mrs. William Bingham and Mrs. Robert Morris, leaders of the younger and older Federalist social sets, to exclude Republican gentlemen. Society became rigidly Federalist at the capital and elsewhere in reaction to the radical, aggressive phase of the French Revolution.[7]

The New Theater on Chestnut Street was completed in time to

become another center of the articulate Federalist social rally. Its managers, Wignell and Reinagle, recruited a brilliant cast of British actors, secured new scenery, and hired a twenty-piece orchestra. The Washingtons and Adamses attended repeatedly. Other boxes were occupied by Cabinet members, federal officials, Senators, Congressmen, and leading Federalist families and guests. Together they presented to the public the physical embodiment of aristocratic Federalism with its beautiful "Ladies" clad in the latest Parisian and London gowns.[8]

Federalism in Philadelphia was expressed also in appreciation and patronage of the artists Charles Willson Peale, Gilbert Stuart (the Federalists' favorite portrait painter), John Trumbull, and James Peale the noted miniaturist.[9] The conservative Federalist reaction was expressed there and elsewhere in attempts to control the colleges and to support Noah Webster's campaign for the reform of grammar and spelling as part of an emerging American language. Washington proposed a national university; while the American Philosophical Society made an award to Samuel Knox of Frederick, Maryland, for his essay demanding that youth be taught to submerge sectional prejudices.[10] Such was the cultural nationalism that Federalist leaders fostered in contrast to King's and the Wolcotts' New England sectionalism, while they avoided involvement in the European conflict.

This was accompanied, however, by a pronounced tendency among the Hamiltonians and the Essex Junto to look to Britain for intellectual models as well as for styles and art. The leadership of Benjamin West, the American Tory, in English painting [11] facilitated such a cultural *rapprochement* despite vivid memories of British ravages during the War of Independence.

Coit was subjected to these influences during his service in Congress, but he exhibited the continuing interest in radical European intellectuals which characterized more liberal Americans. The extent to which his liberalism was supplanted by reactionary models and rigid conformity during 1795–1798 will be ascertained later. His cultural activity and interests during his early years in Congress can now be portrayed.

Two days after the Chestnut Street Theater opened in mid-February 1794 he wrote to his wife, "All the world has been to the play except myself, who have been at home with my Books. I fancied there might seem an impropriety in my going on account of my mother's death. I have my doubts yet whether I ought to go— tell me what you think of it." [12] She approved of his attendance at the theater, which evinced her cultural interests and enlightenment. Traveling troupes of players occasionally performed in New London.

Two weeks later he described the New Theater simply to his son Robert in reply to his questions:

> You cant think what a fine place it is. all lighted up with Candles & Lamps so as to look as light as day—and there are fine paintings which they call the scenery some look like trees & some like houses —and the Music, there are as many as Twenty Fiddles all playing together. I sent your Cousin Fanny one of the plays they act here.[13]

On April 21 he spent the evening with his guests "at the Theatre. We had one of Shakespeare's plays, King Richard," he informed Mrs. Coit, "but it did not please me so much as I thought Shakespeare's must." [14] Theater attendance marked him as a man of culture and taste and demonstrated his congeniality with the upper Federalist world.[15]

Coit was impressed by the Washingtons. In late February he informed Mrs. Coit that he had dined with "the Presdt":

> Had I a talent at description the Scene might amuse you. He has a public dinner once a week, inviting 20 or 30 members of Congress, of course, taking them in turn. The Center of a long table at which we sit is occupied with a panel of Imagery done in plaster of paris or some other thing, placed on salvars which join to one another

LADY WASHINGTON'S RECEPTION
By Daniel Huntington

so as to have the appearance of one piece thus [drawing] These images are Cupids, Goddesses & such kind of Nonsensical things are not good to eat—the eatables being placed around the table. There is room enough however for aplenty. The Dessert according to my fancy should take the place of these Nicknacks, but that is brought on after the solids are removed, consisting of plum pudding, Ice Cream, Tarts, Trifles, etc., etc. Half the good things in a Circle of half a dozen Friends—or in fact a good piece of Roast Beef & Indian Pudding is better.

While this depreciatory conclusion could be attributed to a desire not to arouse Mrs. Coit's envy, he doubtless preferred the less exotic, simpler standards of the Federalist gentry of eastern Connecticut. That he was uninitiated in the beauties of the large porcelain figures in Meissen, Sèvres, or Winchester ware that graced the tables of those following the fashion of the British and French aristocracies was evident.

The next evening he attended "Mme. Washington's Rout, or Levy or Tea Party," he reported:

Rout, I believe is the proper name. This is a ceremonious Business in which the Company make their Bow to her. The Ladies seat themselves and the Gentlemen are standing about the Room in a heap or in smaller Circles as it happens. Tea and Coffee with Cake are handed round, and when you please you quit. I staid only about half an hour. I must go again for I cannot answer one of my Landlady's inquiries about the dress of the Ladies.[16]

Phrased in eastern Connecticut dialect for a wife who regretted that she lacked his education, these descriptions announced to mutual New London friends his participation in the formal rites of Washington's court. Although Coit may have felt somewhat awkward during his first attendance at "Lady" Washington's levee, he bowed to her again at the next one. "I have been this Evening to Madame Washington's Rout. I believe I mentioned this Ceremony to you once before. There was only one Lady to wait on her Ladyship. There were perhaps a dozen Gentlemen. The quality, I fancy had all gone to the play with which I have got surfeited." [17] Thereafter he appears to have regarded his attendance upon the President and "Lady" Washington as a matter of course.

He was much impressed by the fine brick houses in Philadelphia and by the numerous "Chariots, Coaches &c" on the streets. He intended to bring his family there during Congressional sessions but never did. He was enchanted by the model jail, which he inspected and described in a lengthy account to his older brother Daniel.[18] He followed the current fashion when, at Mrs. Coit's request, he had a fine miniature of himself in full front view wearing his dress coat painted by James Peale.[19]

Cautiously, on February 23, 1796, he described the Washington Birthday Celebration and Ball for the edification of his eight-and-a-half-year-old son "Bob," lest he and his mother conclude that he had enjoyed himself unduly while absent from them:

> There has been grand doings here yesterday as you will see by the papers on the President's Birthday—Bells ringing, guns firing & soldiers parading—fine fun for the Boys—& a mighty fine Ball in the Evening at the Amphitheatre—this is a place where Mr. Rickets rides his horses, sometimes with a little Boy standing on his shoulders—the horses in full gallop—the amphitheatre is a round building of—I guess 200 feet Diameter—(if you don't know what that means look in your dictionary) it is built of Brick about 15 foot high. There are Boxes with Seats all round & in the middle it is left open to the ground for him to ride. They had a nice floor laid over it on purpose to dance—& there was room for 200 Couples to dance at once. I was there & saw a deal of fine folks. I wish your Mama could have seen it, or you, but I did not care much about it myself.[20]

Obviously, he had attended the horse shows at the Amphitheatre before.

Since Mrs. Coit was unhappy at their friends' diminished social attentions in New London during his annual absences, he discreetly avoided mention of private social engagements in Philadelphia. These, it may be inferred, were primarily within the Congressional circle. No reference survives of any participation by him in the activities of the gay, heavy-drinking, extravagant, somewhat risqué, and occasionally profane Bingham set, which included only a few Congressmen such as Harrison Gray Otis of Boston (beginning in 1797).[21]

Although he fought the attempt to stampede the United States into war with Britain during the session of 1793–1794, Coit did not surrender to intellectual reaction as did Noah Webster and Wolcott Jr. That season he read the new Philadelphia edition of Mary Wollstonecraft's *Vindication of the Rights of Women*. While doing so, he urged his discontented wife cautiously to develop a certain independence of thought and action, with due respect for his marital superiority. Four years later, with their small daughters' education in mind and on the eve of the X Y Z crisis, he sent her a copy of Erasmus Darwin's *Female Education in Boarding Schools*. Meanwhile, he kept their profile portraits on his desk in his rooms. In February 1795 Coit attended the first sermon in America delivered at Philadelphia by Dr. Joseph Priestley, the noted chemist, political radical, and unitarian.[22]

Participation in Washington's court and Federalist associations in Congress did not diminish Coit's attachment to deism as the appropriate gentleman's religion. Neither the precariousness of life in a city repeatedly afflicted with yellow fever nor antipathy to atheistic Jacobinism precipitated him into the emotional orthodoxy that Timothy Dwight would soon preach at Yale College.

Mrs. Coit's report of a great revival among the Baptists and "the great dipping" at New London in early March 1794 surprised him because "awakenings of the sort appear not to have been common of late." He had little faith in them, although he was glad that they made "the subjects better members of society or happier people." He was "satisfied" that "These operations fancied to be the work of the Spirit of God are . . . mere worship of the Imagination," excited by the "Passions." "I hope you will not catch the religious frenzy which by your letters appears to be raging." [23]

He continued in an eloquent statement of his faith in the God of Nature:

> I cannot believe that the Supreme Being, the first trait of whose Character as it must be conceived of by every reasonable man must be benevolence, ever could make our acceptance with him depend on hidden and mistical operations not within the reach of our natural powers. You'll be pleased if you read a sermon of my favorite Yorks on Enthusiasm. He paints the powers of Imagination in lively and forceable Colours, & to my fancy gives a juster view of Religious Character & Duties than many graver writers. What are the powers which heaven has given us? Are they not merely to fulfill the Duties it has assigned to us in Society? And in what of our actions can we suppose the Supreme being to be pleased but in those which tend to promote our happiness & that of those about us. Our Devotions, can they be profitable to our maker? On the contrary can they rationally be pointed to any other view than our own improvement by leading us to reflect on our Situation & by contemplating our Duties to warn us in the pursuit of them.[24]

Returning to the subject in late April, he assured his wife that her "melancholly Impressions . . . have no foundation in Nature," and that "on trifling occasions" it "would be totally inconsistent with rational Ideas" of the nature of "The Supreme Being" to "make such discoveries" of "the pages of futurity to the minds of Men":

> His wisdom has fixed the world & its movements in general Laws. Those Laws we get an imperfect knowledge of by observation & Experience, but this knowledge thus obtained is the only guide we have. Carefully attended to 'tis enough, I hope, to lead us quickly thro' the path of Life & although that path has some thorns in its way yet it has its Roses.[25]

When her premonitions of an early death recurred two years later during the Congressional crisis precipitated by ratification of Jay's Treaty, he repudiated the Calvinist "apprehension of an angry god preparing endless miseries in . . . a life beyond this . . . for the greater part of the human Race & which could be avoided only by some misterious change to be wrought in the mind by means not in our power to command, & the existence of which must almost necessarily be a matter of doubt to the person who had been the subject of it." "These theories," he added, "I believe are as false as they are distressing. They are inconsistent with any Ideas I can form of the benevolence of Deity and to me incredible." [26]

Coit continued, then, despite the developing reaction, to be a child of the Enlightenment, with its faith in science, reason, progress, and a benevolent deity. To this he linked a Federalist's appreciation of "passion's" obstacle to reason's expression in human affairs, and the belief in "social station" that was so popular in the Standing Order. He elaborated this view in a manner congenial to liberal Federalism as he analyzed Mary Wollstonecraft's *Vindication* for the benefit of his wife during his Congressional session:

> Her book . . . is certainly wrote in a bold nervous and manly stile. She soars above vulgar prejudices & appears to rise on no feeble wings. 'tis visionary to expect the world while civilization continues will in all things be guided by right reason. The fabrick of Society is not formed by reflection but fashion, habit & a variety of accidental causes have a hand in the Constitution of it & it is a mixture of virtue & vice, wisdom & folly. Yet its vices may be in some degree repressed & its follies may in some measure be corrected; Minds which are superior to the Shackles of Fashion will sometimes point out brilliant improvements, their lights may help in forming of individual Characters, but the world at large is not so easily mended.[27]

Other letters to her expressed a well-defined agrarianism. Although superficially similar to that of the Physiocrats, this probably originated in Connecticut with the Reverend Jared Eliot. Further-

more, appreciation of New London's exposed position in case of a
conflict with Great Britain or France led Coit to enlarge upon the
virtues of farm life as he urged his wife to repair with their children to his newly acquired Montville farm.

Rather than political ambition—which he disclaimed as his leading motive in life—his chief desire, he said, was to achieve "Independence." This would make them both happy by providing the
means to gratify "our wants." This was his chief motive, he insisted,
for wishing to live on a farm. In February 1796, when the Republicans in Congress threatened to revive the Anglo-American crisis, he
wrote her:

> Possibly my schemes of a Country Life are utopian but I hope to
> have the opportunity to try them, and that they will not prove so.
> My last will have satisfied you on the subject of the Montville farm.
> May I hope from what you say of Submission &c that I shall find
> some degree of acquiescence. At least that you will be disposed to
> make the best & not the worst of what may appear unavoidable.[28]

In similar adherence to the lingering English tradition that determined the mode of life of the successful man, George Cabot had
retired to his Brookline estate from Beverly, Massachusetts.

However, Coit's wife won the argument. He disposed of his two-
acre place with house and outbuildings "pleasantly situated in New
London," probably to her relative Charles Bulkeley. However, the
buildings on the nine-hundred-acre livestock farm that he acquired
in Montville were so old, and the style of house his wife desired
was so expensive, that he sold the farm to Major Hillhouse. He
then purchased and removed to an acre property on the "Highway
within the city limits" adjacent to her brother's home. There he was
able to enjoy nature and experiment with Lombardy poplars and
the new grasses, while Nancy found satisfaction in the close proxim-
ity of relatives and the social life of the port. But he continued to

dream of farm life and of practicing the improved methods that the Connecticut Agricultural Society propagated.[29]

His deism and modified rationalism made it consistent for him to be interested in the plans to organize a Masonic lodge in New London before he returned to Congress in the autumn of 1794. Many leaders of the American Revolution had been Masons. Deism, which they favored, was at the height of its popularity. In July, therefore, Samuel Green, printer of the *Connecticut Gazette* and a member of the First Church who subsequently became its deacon, serialized Thomas Paine's aggressively deist and sensational *Age of Reason* in the *Gazette* while advertising *The Free-Mason's Pocket Companion.*[30]

These actions, Green's influence, and Coit's quiet interest and promise to assist led to the organization of the Union Lodge of Freemasons in New London. When Mrs. Coit reiterated vigorously her objections to his involvement in it, he replied tactfully from Philadelphia that had he known she was "so seriously & unalterably discomposed about the paltry subject" he would "have had nothing further to do with it as you must know I am a Novice in the business." He reassured her with an urbane semiphilosophical description of the nature of Freemasonry:

> It is merely a combination for the purposes of friendship & humanity. But why, you ask then these airs of mistery? You must seek for the Reason of them in the human Mind which is oftentimes strongly influenced & affected by mere mechanical considerations. The general principles of Benevolence & humanity bind the whole family of Man together & should make Men a family of Brothers. Yet the distinctions of country & of party place barriers between them & raise sentiments of hostility in their minds equal or superior to what one would expect to find had they been formed by the hand of nature from different materials & with natural principles of mutual hostility. The virtuous & the good however it should seem would find principles

of mutual attraction in their virtues. Yet how feeble are the attach-
ments of mankind when no other Considerations combine them but
a mutual respect to their virtues. When & where originated this In-
stitution it is impossible since everything of any considerable antiquity
has its origin involved in obscurity to tell. Like all others it is capable
of abuse, . . . Yet its design and general tendency is beneficial—
it is a kind of artificial strengthening to principles of benevolence &
humanity & deserves at worst to be regarded as trifling.[31]

Coit's philosophical approach to Freemasonry was character-
istically tolerant and cosmopolitan. However, it is evident from
this statement that despite his friendship with Noah Webster his
practice of that grammarian's precepts was imperfect. This was not
unusual at that time for men of his "station."

Coit joined the Union Lodge, of which Amasa Learned was also
a founder. On June 30, 1796, their pastor, the Reverend Henry Channing, addressed it on "the Minister of the Benevolent Jesus." He developed the theme that the Christian man "cultivates universal
benevolence," a deist concept, before admonishing the members not
to frequent the taverns too avidly after meetings. Coit and Elias
Perkins then thanked him for "his discourse—this day" as the
Lodge's Committee.[32]

Although he was determined not to allow Nancy to dominate
him or to surrender to melancholia during his absences, Coit regarded her with genuine affection and unusual respect. He conferred
with her while instructing her from a distance about the training of
their children. He enjoyed her regular letters, replying in kind to her
and Robert. He was glad when their friends paid her social attentions. He sent the children pictures and "Conversation Cards," and
urged her during his later Congresional terms to hold whist parties,
for which he sent her playing cards. While cultivating "the politeness" that enabled him to overlook her "faults" and to correct his
own, he enjoyed her poetry, stimulated her intellectual development,
briefed her on the major diplomatic crises as they occurred, and

thus cultivated her "fortitude" should threatened wars materialize. He relied upon Nancy to hand his regular, anonymous Congressional "Newspaper Letter" to the *Gazette.*

Interestingly, he suggested that she accept his cheerful philosophy of duty and "Content" with one's "station" in life. He urged that she apply to their personal relationship and other spheres Aristotle's Golden Mean. He encouraged her to develop resourcefulness in harmony with their interdependence and "those passions and feelings from whence the most refined enjoyments of Life proceed." To her and Bob he made it clear that he preferred life with them in New London to prolonged absences in Philadelphia while attending Congress. He wrote her repeatedly of his longing for the end of each session, when he could catch the first stage for New York City and New London.[33]

As "Dr. Nancy" matured, he entrusted her with increased responsibility for their domestic and his non-legal affairs when he was absent. He authorized Perkins to draw upon her for his subscription to the stock of the Niantic drawbridge, in financing which he had joined him and forty-three others in supplement to the proceeds of the lottery authorized by the legislature. He instructed the Union Bank to pay to her the March first semiannual dividends upon his stock. Such experience in the management of their affairs was invaluable to her when his sudden death in 1798 left her responsible for rearing and educating their children.[34]

To Nancy he confided also his philosophy of political courage during the protest raised in New London against Jay's mission to London by such friends as Captain Bulkeley because of bitterness at the British seizures of Connecticut vessels. A man, Coit informed her on May 1, 1794:

> . . . should carry the Rule of his Conduct in his own Bosom. This is a guide which may mislead but can never deceive him. . . . I have no doubt of B's friendship nor am I offended at his message; harder words than those he uses have been so common on this subject

that those sound very civil. When Madness & Pride claim to themselves exclusively the praise of Courage, epithets of Timidity become honourable. To bear injuries with temper, to seek with coolness & moderation the best means of redressing the wrongs of a Nation are actions which I think a man need not be ashamed of.[35]

Thus during his first Congressional session he expressed his maxim of calm, independent moderation as the best mode of advancing the national interest. It would guide him thenceforth irrespective of partisan storms.

Subsequently, he shared with Bob his own intellectual and literary interests as the boy approached the teens. He was interested in his study of Latin and then of Greek. They agreed that the title of Abbé Reynal's *Histoire des Deux Indies* was a misnomer. He enjoined Bob that "the mode of speaking by most practiced speakers is the proper one & the best—the same with regard to writing." He gave him *The Spectator* and volumes of poetry including "young's Night Thoughts and Milton's paradise lost."

As the boy reached twelve, Coit shared with him his interest in agriculture. He sent him "Lucerne Seed" from Philadelphia for an experimental planting, to be shared with "your Unkle Hallam if he is a mind to try it, & if he is give him half of the seed." In return, Bob reported in detail on the progress of his garden, where peanuts and rice were planted to vary the customary radishes, peas, corn, and potatoes. Coit sent him the Philadelphia newspapers as the Naval War with France began after the X Y Z affair. Such was his cultivation of the character and intellect of his oldest son, who was later to have a notable banking career in New London.[36]

From Philadelphia during Congressional sessions Coit also corresponded with his New London associates. He confided Congressional news occasionally to Bulkeley, upon whom he relied to pick up additional stock in the Union Bank for him "at or under 80." [37] He wrote more regularly to Elias Perkins, his letters supplementing the compressed, objective report of Congressional proceedings that he supplied the *Gazette*. Both were undoubtedly appreciated by the mercantile and agricultural communities of eastern Connecticut.

Coit sided with the New London bankers and merchants in their vain opposition to the chartering of a rival bank in Norwich in 1796. His reasons were admittedly selfish, in part because he did not think there was sufficient business for two banks "on terms either beneficial to themselves or the public." However, he was motivated also by realistic appreciation of the dangers inherent in the "immense Effect of the European war . . . on this Country—the Spirit of Commercial Enterprise & Speculation has arisen to a heigth [*sic*] probably never before attained in this Country—& on the cessation of the War very important Changes—probably deep bankruptcies must take place." This justified, he said, "a kind of guardianship over Mercantile Speculation" by refusing "aid" to the proposed Norwich bank.[38] Sharing as this view did Oliver Wolcott Jr.'s appreciation of the dangers already inherent in the speculative bubble that would ruin many important Federalist merchants and speculators within two years,[39] it evinced Coit's foresight as well as his practical flair that made him highly regarded as a Congressman.

CHAPTER FIVE

Stability During Crisis

COIT's calm, independent judgment and self-control were among his chief assets in Congress. Undoubtedly they enabled him to exert a stabilizing influence upon New London during the late summer and early autumn of 1794, when the Whiskey Insurrection in western Pennsylvania against the federal excise alarmed Connecticut. Senator Ellsworth, who regarded the Federal Union at best as unstable and temporary, feared that discontented elements in "the Eastern quarter" might be aroused to similar action by the Democratic Clubs. Although a few lawyers in Connecticut, "taking their tone from New Haven," attempted "to agitate" it, their effort was "unsuccessful" and had to be "abandoned." President Washington led an army into the Pittsburgh area, assisted by Hamilton and Wolcott Jr., restored order there, and calmed New England.

Although the August–September crisis passed quickly, when Coit and Learned returned to Philadelphia in early November they found the Administration determined to discourage further activity of the Clubs. To them Washington attributed responsibility for the futile uprising.[1]

While the House was perfecting its reply to the President's annual address, Coit voted with the majority for an amendment that asserted this responsibility pointedly. The President's disapproval of "self-created societies" in his message and Congressional concurrence so discredited the Clubs that they lapsed into inactivity, as Coit had predicted to Perkins they would.[2]

Then Hamilton's announcement that he would resign from the Treasury Department on January 31, 1795, after this signal vindication of federal authority, enabled Coit to express his appreciation of the great Secretary's services to his young friend:

> The Government has I have no doubt owed much to the Vigour & Energy of that man's mind, & has had in him a most able faithfull and indefatigable Servant; our affairs have got in so good a train he may not be so much mist out of the Administration as he would have been at an earlier period—his abilities however have been & are so distinguished that a well wisher to the Government without particular prejudices cannot fail to regret that he is leaving us.

He predicted accurately that Oliver Wolcott Jr. "will probably succeed him." This event enhanced Connecticut's influence in the Administration and strengthened that official's influence in the state.[3]

There wasn't a great deal of business before Congress, Coit reported. The revenues sufficed to pay the expenses of suppressing the Insurrection. He was kept busy with committee assignments, while residing in the same rooming house with Griswold, Swift, Tracy, and Senator Ellsworth. He informed Perkins of his brother Elijah's inclination in Philadelphia "to Democracy," and wished for an early peace in Europe so as to give the French an opportunity to draft a constitution unembarrassed by crisis. He added, significantly:

> More & More people are giving up their hopes of them from the continued train of Revolutions in which their Councils have been revolving, & I confess I have my fears they will not eventually get a Government that will pay them for the Evils that have attended the Revolution—but I do not wholly despair—less of despotism than they have had would not perhaps have answered the purpose of defending them against their Enemies, the cruelty & madness which has accompanied it was perhaps the natural growth of the necessity of the occasion & dissolution of former Establishments.[4]

This was far more tolerant and understanding of France's difficulties than the Wolcotts' Gallophobia.

During early January, the House debated on whether or not European nobles immigrating to the United States should renounce their titles upon admission to citizenship. Congress' decision to require this, Coit believed, would please Captain Bulkeley "& some friends on the Bank" in New London. However, he reported to him, "You'll see all the Connecticut members for the Nobles but I suppose you'll say they could not help it. Col. Wadsworth bid them vote so."[5] Evidently that ex-Congressman, director of the Bank of United States, and speculator in federal securities exerted greater influence than has been supposed. That Coit voted with his delegation to allow the nobles to retain their titles after naturalization disclosed a hitherto unsuspected penchant for aristocracy, such as the Essex Junto openly avowed.

As a champion of the maritime "interest" and chairman of a select committee, Coit reported a bill to secure state cession of lands needed for lighthouses, public piers, buoys, etc.

Simultaneously, he was introduced to the corrupt influence that aggressive land speculators were exerting that season in American legislatures. In Augusta, Georgia, Senator James Gunn, Associate Justice of the Supreme Court James Wilson, other federal judges, and influential speculator groups corruptly purchased the huge Yazoo lands from the Georgia legislature in a nation-wide scandal. This besmirched the reputation of such leading Federalists as Wilson, Congressman Robert Goodloe Harper of South Carolina, and Robert Morris.[6]

In late December 1794, a smaller, less influential speculator clique, represented by Robert Randall and Charles Whitney, attempted to bribe Congressmen of both political parties so as to secure a grant of from eleven to twenty million acres of Indian lands comprising most of present-day lower Michigan. The consideration offered to the Congressmen was marketable shares in the land grant, after the technique of the Yazoo lobbyists at Augusta. Colonel Ethan Allan, certain Massachusetts capitalists, and Detroit Indian traders and speculators figured in this attempted coup at the expense of the national domain and the integrity of Congress. Interestingly, when it was exposed in the House, the culprits received extraordinarily gentle treatment. Only Randall and Whitney were arrested and brought before the House in a sensational scene. They had made the actual overtures, which had produced signed contracts with a dozen or more members, before Congressman William Smith rose and described their attempts to bribe him.[7]

Coit was a member of the bipartisan Committee of Privileges to which the case of Randall and Whitney was referred. The account of this assignment, when published in the Connecticut papers together with the details of the scandal, undoubtedly enhanced his reputation at home. Until January 1796, the Committee and the House devoted an undue amount of time to the matter, while the culprits were kept in custody only sporadically by the sergeant at arms. Members of the House who were parties to contracts with the speculators escaped punishment by claiming that they had signed only as a means of securing concrete evidence of the attempt to bribe Congress. Whitney's profession of innocence of any improper action, while he identified the organizers of the project before the bar of the House after the manner of a state's witness, resulted in a light punishment. He and his collaborator were released by the Speaker after the House ruled that they had been imprisoned sufficiently already for contempt. They were obliged, however, to face the federal court.

To Perkins, Coit depreciated the entire matter after its conclusion, while conveying an inside view of the inquiry. "It was a paltry piece of business," he wrote in a manner that suggested an attempt to expunge the stigma that the episode had attached to the reputation of the House, "some of the Gentlemen to whom the application was made had *pretended to listen* to his offers to *draw* Randall explicitly & unequivocally to commit an offence for which they moved to punish him, & others jealous from his Story that he had bribed some of the members, from an anxiety to find out the Secret." [8] Although some members of the House were very indignant at the attempt, it is evident that Coit, like other Federalist legislators of that year, perceived but dimly its grave implications for public ethics. If the coup had succeeded, it would have produced a gigantic fraud as scandalous and with as decisive political consequences as the Yazoo land companies perpetrated in Georgia.

The treaty that Jay had negotiated with Great Britain, although signed on November 19, 1794, did not arrive until after Coit returned home from the short session. This postponed a recurrence of the partisan conflict that had preceded Jay's departure for London. During that short session, Coit supported the abortive attempt to create a federal "Legion" of 4800 men for three years. In this action he shared the New England Federalists' desire for a standing army. He was at home in New London when a leak from the Senate during the new treaty's consideration precipitated a stormy protest against its injury to the Franco-American alliance and to American interests. This was intensified by its ratification on June 22 at Washington's insistence. [9]

No expression of Coit's at that time disclosed any of the growing prejudice against the South that was expressed by the Wolcotts and younger Connecticut Wits as that region made an extremely heated protest against Jay's Treaty. This document established a commission to settle the compensation due British creditors because of some states' interference with the collection of pre-Revolutionary private American debts, inferentially required their payment, and validated the highly unpopular Fairfax and Granville land titles in Virginia and North Carolina, while it secured to slaveholders no compensation for three thousand slaves carried away in 1783 by the evacuating British armies. North *and* South resented the unchecked impressment of American seamen and the continued closure of the British West Indies to American trade that followed the

Senate's rejection of the inadequate provision for its opening to small American vessels.

So shrill and vituperative was the agitation against the treaty in the South and among Northern Irish-Americans that Ellsworth and other Connecticut leaders were alarmed. Dr. Lemuel Hopkins, a lesser Wit, remarked to the new Secretary of the Treasury, "There are at all times certain portions of this our globe from whence useful lessons . . . arise. Such at present are *France* & the *United States,* or rather NEW ENGLAND (for the southern states I regard as a chaos of animated atoms)." [10]

Noah Webster warned Wolcott Jr. that violence might be anticipated in the South, from which he predicted the Northern states would eventually have to separate since it appeared that the former "are to be governed very much by the French nation." [11] Yet anti-treaty mobs in Boston at that time were destroying the property of foreigners, a circumstance that to the unprejudiced should have indicated that violence was not peculiarly Southern. Commercial and shipping interests were especially aggrieved at the treaty provisions for countervailing British duties, which nullified the favorable effects of the American Navigation Acts so far as the British merchant marine was concerned.

Strenuously successful attempts were made in the *Connecticut Courant* by contributing essayists to convince the freemen that the treaty contained "the best Terms" obtainable as the result of "an able negotiation." Wolcott Jr. expressed his pleasure to Congressman Benjamin Goodhue of Salem "that New England remains firm & composed." He added significantly, "If the extravagances which are fashionable in the other parts of our country were to extend to the Northern States, our liberties would soon be lost." [12]

That summer's popular protest against the treaty was preliminary to a prolonged conflict when Congress reconvened in late November, sullen, "preparing for battle," as Wolcott Jr. informed the incredulous Wadsworth. The Republican majority in the House sought to prevent the enforcement of Jay's Treaty by withholding the necessary appropriations. This stratagem presented a major constitutional issue and challenged the Northern maritime, shipbuilding, commercial, and manufacturing interests, a portion of which had been critical of the treaty. They were now united in favor of "fulfilling it." [13]

If the Republicans had succeeded in their object, they would have rendered future treaty-making extremely complicated and would have revived the acute Anglo-American crisis of 1794, with the difference arising from General Wayne's defeat of the northwestern Indians. This had made inevitable Britain's surrender of the fur-trading posts to the United States. The Republicans were making large gains by appealing to anti-British popular prejudices, to Southern opposition to the payment of the pre-Revolutionary debts and compensation to British creditors, and to urban resentment at the continued impressment of American seamen. Jefferson's followers were attempting to entice the commercial farmers from their support of the Federalist Party, a maneuver which, if successful, would overturn the domestic balance of political power.

At that time in the Fourth Congress the balance between the parties was held by a bipartisan group of moderates. Swift of Connecticut was such a moderate. Of the other Connecticut men, Goodrich and the freshmen Dana and Davenport voted consistently Federalist as followers of the Wolcott faction. Coit, Griswold, and Nathaniel Smith, another freshman, voted at least once with the Republicans.

A decided majority in the House opposed the Administration largely because of the treaty. Legislative action depended upon persuading the moderates to support individual measures on their merits. At first the representatives marked time, awaiting formal British ratification so that the President might "lay the treaty before us," as Coit informed Perkins, legatee and nephew of the wealthy merchant, the late Thomas Shaw of New London. The Connecticut delegation's chief interim business was the consideration and rejection of the demand of United States District Judge for Connecticut, Richard Law, that his salary be increased. Coit attempted to interject careful economy into construction of the public buildings in the new capital city of Washington, to which the federal government would remove in 1801.[14]

Washington then requested simultaneous fulfillment of the new treaties with Spain, Algiers, and Britain. The first two were quite popular, but the House's attitude toward the latter was well defined. As Coit reported to Perkins:

> If our Act was necessary to give it being it would not be—or if an act of ours could kill it such is generally calculated to be our Complexion, it would probably live but a little while; fixed, however, as are the barriers of the Constitution—the U S Senate having the Power to make the Compact by which the national faith is pledged & nothing being left with us but to withhold our Concurrence to acts that may be necessary to carry the Compact into Effect, it seems pretty doubtfull what feasible ground the opponents of ye Treaty in our house can take; The President & Senate will I presume proceed to do what on their part can be done to carry the Treaty into Effect—the British will I believe deliver the Posts & tho' late & with an ill grace the House of Representatives will I fancy, finally concur in doing what is to be done on their part—better late than never.

He then observed irrelevantly that Senator Ellsworth's recent appointment as Chief Justice of the Supreme Court of the United States "removes one of the list of Candidates you gave me for Govr. shall we have a Senator sent on in his Room or will the Executive wait for the Sessions of Assembly?"[15] Coit was maintaining an active interest in Connecticut politics.

His position became of vital importance to the Administration's attempt to secure House cooperation in the fulfillment of Jay's Treaty. The Republicans' attempt to prevent this occupied most of the time between March 7 and April 30, 1796. They began on the earlier date with Edward Livingston's Resolution. This requested that the President lay before the House his instructions to Jay and the correspondence of his mission. Jay had been *persona non grata* to the Southern Congressmen when appointed, no doubt because of his pro-Northern course during the controversial Jay-Gardoqui negotiations of 1786. The Resolution was an attempt to fish in troubled waters.

Implicitly it claimed for the House a share in the treaty-making power, which the Constitution reserved to the President with the advice and consent of the Senate. The maneuver was so popular in the House that it alarmed Oliver Ellsworth. It precipitated a long, vituperative, and frequently irrelevant debate. The chief issue was James Madison's and Albert Gallatin's claim that the House possessed discretionary authority, analogous to that of the British House of Commons, derived from the legislative and money-appropriating functions, to exercise its judgment as to whether or not to assist in carrying any treaty into effect. This embarrassed Anglophile Administration supporters. The Federalists were obliged to debate the constitutional issue and in so doing to discuss the treaty's provisions, with some of which they were at variance.[16]

Coit's only diversion before the Resolution came to a vote was his service on the Committee of Privileges, which considered Senator Gunn's challenge to the Georgia member Abraham Baldwin arising from the latter's criticism of the Yazoo frauds. This raised anew the problem of how to exclude dueling from Congress, which the House solved by obliging Gunn to apologize for violating its rule against this. The debate on Livingston's Resolution Coit held would "decide no principle." Interjection of "important principles" into the discussion would only prolong it. Two weeks of Republican attacks mustered such support for Livingston's motion that Washington wrote Hamilton on March 22 for advice on how to deal with such a request.

On that same day Coit delivered a long speech on the points at issue after ridiculing the lies circulated against Jay's Treaty. Private talk of an impeachment had disclosed the real motive for the request for the papers, he asserted, despite Livingston's partial denial of such intent in reply to a query of Tracy's. Coit then upheld the Constitution's allocation of the treaty-making power vigorously. The Resolution was unconstitutional since it encroached upon "the rights of other branches of the Government." Only if the House shared the treaty-making power would it have the right to demand the relevant papers. No sound reason had been offered to justify this. Instead of British Parliamentary precedents cited by the Republicans, Coit insisted that in the Confederation would be found the relevant historical background of the treaty-making power.

Regardless of Madison's recently expressed doubts, he declared that a treaty made in accord with the Constitution was "the law of the land," as binding as treaties had been when concluded under the Articles of Confederation. Stronger arguments than those as yet presented were necessary to convince him that the Constitution conferred upon the House any authority derived from British precedents. In reply to another Republican argument, he declared that the nation's representation in the Senate was as complete as it was "in the House"; nor was the latter "the popular branch of Government" analogous to the House of Commons, as the Virginians contended. He did not doubt that "the powers vested by the Constitution were well vested." Adoption of the Resolution would not decide the controverted issue, and if the House insisted upon its request "he was happy that the Constitution was not wholly in their hands." Sounder and blunter words in support of the Constitution and Washington's administration could not have been spoken.[17]

Following him, James Hillhouse of Connecticut developed the same position. The other Connecticut men except Swift joined in opposing the Resolution. Despite their efforts it was adopted by the large majority of 61 to 38. Nevertheless, their sturdy defense of the Administration and the Constitution increased Congressman Chauncey Goodrich's "esteem" for his fellow Representatives "every day," he informed his father-in-law the Lieutenant Governor.[18] While awaiting the President's reply to the Resolution, which Livingston and Gallatin handed him, Coit observed that it was preliminary to the "main Treaty question," when the constitutional issue would necessarily recur.[19]

Courteously but forcefully, Washington refused to transmit the requested papers. After referring to his participation in the Federal Convention, he declared that the Constitution had wisely delegated treaty-making to the President with the advice and consent of the small Senate, since secrecy in negotiation was necessary.[20] Coit was pleased with this reiteration of his own position. He and the other Connecticut men voted against reference of Washington's reply to the Committee of the Whole. To Perkins he remarked on April 6:

> I fancy you were pleased with the president's answer to our demand for papers it is certainly very well done. Whether our people will be for answering it by putting resolutions expressing different opinions on the Journals or how I cannot say. I pray God the British have not been Rascals enough to treat a discretion with some officers of theirs here to deliver the posts or not on the 1st June according to the disposition of the Treaty; if so we may have trouble yet—if not & the posts are delivered—all I think will very clearly be well.[21]

On the next day, he voted against the Blount resolutions without knowing that Madison was their author. As adopted, these asserted bluntly the Madison-Gallatin thesis of a House discretionary right to deliberate "on the expediency or inexpediency of carrying such treaty into effect, and to determine and act thereon, as, in their judgment, may be most conductive to the public good"; and, second, that it was not essential to the propriety of any House application for papers to the President "for information desired by them" to state "in the application the purpose for which the information is desired." [22]

On April 8, during an interval in the debate on the enforcement of the treaty, Coit departed from Federalist policy to support Gallatin and the Republicans in their futile attempt to reduce the number of frigates to be completed for the new navy from three to two, as a committee had recommended. His reasons, although unstated, were probably derived from the Treasury's straitened resources. This James Holland gave as his reason for voting against the supplementary Naval Armament bill that Coit also opposed. Goodrich had remarked earlier that the "obvious" course toward the navy was "to equip two ships for protecting our harbours from petty insults and privateers" and "to lay up" the remaining shipbuilding materials.[23]

Coit's action on this measure, together with his temporary liaison with the opposition party, provoked the Secretary of the Treasury's displeasure. The New Londoner's leadership in the Connecticut delegation's fight against Livingston's Resolution might have led him to expect advancement to the Senate to fill the seat left vacant by Ellsworth's elevation to the Supreme Court. However, ten days after Coit's vote on Gallatin's side to reduce the frigates to two, Wolcott Jr. advised his father the Lieutenant Governor that it was "important that the good old habits of Connecticut should be maintained. Among these habits, that of promoting men in regular gradation is the best." Since all "members of the old Connecticut representation" in Congress "have acquitted themselves well; there is, therefore, no principle upon which a preference can be made among them except talents and seniority." A month later, the legislature at Hartford elevated Hillhouse, Timothy Dwight's brother-in-law, to the Senate! [24]

Immediately before this, Coit delivered a major speech. This supported the Sedgwick Resolution pledging fulfillment of Jay's Treaty, while Hartford merchants were meeting to express their

"Fears of Ruin, should the provision for carrying" it "into effect be refused" as part of a national mercantile campaign in behalf of the Treaty. Previously, Coit had done his best to persuade the House to act expeditiously in giving effect to all three new treaties. Now, after supporting Hillhouse's untenable invocation of international law and the rights of man to invalidate the Southern claim for compensation for the slaves carried off in 1783,[25] he attempted tactfully to draw the moderates from their liaison with the extreme Republicans and gain their support for execution of Jay's Treaty.

He upheld that document article by article despite a privately expressed distaste for its disadvantages. He maintained that British abandonment of the claim for compensation for expropriated Tory property had been balanced in negotiation of the Treaty of Paris against a withdrawal of the American claim for the slaves seized before then, citing John Adams as his authority. International law, Coit declared correctly, did not uphold the tenet "free ships make free goods," which Britain had refused to accept. Coit tacitly supported the United States' acquiescence in the harsher British maritime code for the duration of the war. Compensation for "lawful impediments" preventing collection of the pre-Revolutionary debts would be paid by the United States government, he said, rather than by individual debtors after the mixed commission's award. The official contraband list in the treaty was "highly favourable to the United States," Coit asserted, undoubtedly because Britain would pay for provisions when seized as contraband. Other important advantages were the opening of the East Indies trade and surrender of the Northwest posts, he asserted soundly. A more favorable treaty could not have been secured in existing circumstances, he added realistically in contradiction to the views of some merchants.

He riddled sarcastically Madison's claim that a treaty submitted to the House was "a mere treaty in negociation." This claim implied that the House could stipulate changes in its terms, and, he

OLIVER WOLCOTT JR.
By James Steward, ca. 1805

added in a *reductio ad absurdum,* even send its own minister extraordinary to the other nation to secure them! "He would like to see the gentleman from Virginia, . . . wrapt in his mantle of doubts and problems, and going on a mission to the Court of London to clear up the business," Coit remarked ironically. What "would be the situation of the country in case the treaty should be rejected," which the Republicans hinted the House might do. The Anglo-American crisis would recur and lead "infallibly" to war, since "it is hardly to be expected that the American people are going to sit down quietly and without compensations, under the injuries they have sustained" from vessel seizures under the Orders in Council. Furthermore, it "would be absurd to think of further negociations" if the House prevented the treaty's execution. American "passion, pride and ambition not interest," he predicted, would lead to a declaration of war against Britain after such an action. And such a war, he predicted, would lead inevitably to a dissolution of the government of the United States. The wisdom of non-involvement in the European conflict was Coit's most cogent plea for treaty enforcement, at it had been Hamilton's when securing Jay's mission and a continuance of friendly Anglo-American relations that were so essential to the American fiscal system. America's interest and its pledged word, Coit urged forcefully, should persuade the House to adopt the Sedgwick Resolution, which he was confident that it would do.[26]

Careful, legalistic, classic in its logic, abreast of international law, based upon the records of the Versailles negotiation, realistic, calm, constitutionally sound, this argument was much more favorable to Jay's Treaty than the appraisals of present-day historians. Coit necessarily omitted mention—if he knew of it—of Hamilton's secret advance assurance to Lord Grenville, British Secretary of State for Foreign Affairs, that the United States would not declare war upon Great Britain if the negotiation should fail. This had handicapped Jay during the negotiations and prevented him from attempting to force a modification of Britain's harsh maritime code in behalf of the United States by threatening American adherence to the Armed Neutrality.[27] Coit's object was to prevent an Anglo-American war by securing enforcement of the treaty, which would have been impossible had Hamilton's maneuver been divulged.

Furthermore, the Treaty secured to American vessel owners compensation for British spoliations by means of a mixed commission, which undoubtedly influenced Coit's view of it. This had been conceded during the negotiation, plus concomitant modification of the Orders in Council, in exchange for the mixed commission to arrange compensation to British creditors for official American interference with the collection of pre-Revolutionary debts. Anti-treaty Southerners could argue plausibly that indirectly *Northern shipowners and merchants were to be compensated for their losses at the expense of all taxpayers, including the pro-French Southerners.* For the Northern Federalists, this was not without humor. So viewed, the treaty brought solid satisfaction to the maritime interests. Equally understandable was the fury of Madison and the Southern Republicans, since their hated British creditors and the British merchant monopolists of their staple markets received their due. The Treaty could also have been viewed, as it was in Paris, as retaliation for Genêt's insulting intrigues. Coit's speech was followed by the Republican Samuel Smith's acceptance of the treaty under Maryland pressure, a crucial break in the opposition.

After an additional week, "poor and emaciated with disease," Fisher Ames concluded the debate with an extraordinary speech in behalf of the Treaty. The Sedgwick Resolution was then carried by the closest margin under the pressure of the petition campaign. After a tie, the vote of the Chairman enabled the Committee of the Whole to report it to the House favorably.

When the known views of absent members were considered, it was evident that a majority in the House opposed the Treaty's enforcement. Coit and the entire Connecticut delegation voted for the

Resolution, after opposing a last-minute attempt to amend it with the statement that while the Treaty was "highly objectionable" it was expedient to carry it into effect. Had Coit been disposed to bend to the popular storm of opposition to John Jay and his treaty, here was a classic opportunity to hedge. He could have changed sides and cast the decisive vote in favor of this searing amendment with its implied criticism of the Administration. Instead, he stood firm with the other Northern Federalists, secured a tie vote, and enabled Speaker Dayton to defeat the amendment with his vote. The Resolution was then adopted by the close vote of 51 to 48. A few days later the House voted $80,000 to fulfill the Treaty.[28]

Thus war with Great Britain was averted by a narrow margin again, and a firm precedent was established for House appropriation of funds necessary for a treaty's enforcement. To this Coit's contributions were notable. An uneasy commercial entente ensued. The French Republic was alienated by this development, resentful of America's abandonment of "free ships make free goods," and injured by Britain's ability to prevent American provisioning of the French West Indies and France by enforcing the Rule of 1756 that prohibited during war a trade banned by France herself during peace.

Although Britain's continued impressment of American seamen handicapped the provisioning of her own armies by American vessels (a policy that was resented by and inexplicable to the Federalist leaders), the Connecticut freemen, merchants, and their Representatives were satisfied. The entire Congressional delegation was nominated for re-election in the Nutmeg State. In October, as the legislature elected Tracy, a Yale and Litchfield Law School classmate of Wolcott Jr., to the Senate, the freemen re-elected the others to Congress. Coit was second highest on the list, below Roger Griswold, Wolcott Jr.'s cousin and Senator Hillhouse's cousin, whose rising star now passed his. Since the Wolcotts were widely influential in Connecticut, invocation of seniority by Wolcott Jr. had prevented Coit's elevation to the Senate. That would have been justified otherwise by his calm, cogent leadership in the fight to vindicate the President's treaty-making power and to enforce Jay's Treaty. This had been fully reported, as had been his vote on the completion of the frigates, in the *Courant* and the *Gazette*.

If Coit had been a graduate of Yale College and Litchfield Law School, his prospects for political advancement would have been rosier in 1795. As matters stood in a state dominated by the alumni of those institutions when they worked together under the Wolcotts' leadership, his Harvard College training, eastern Connecticut background, and independent judgment gave him the wrong ticket in the political lottery.[29]

CHAPTER SIX

Independent Federalist

Joshua Coit's liberalism differentiated him from the Yale-Litchfield men who were assuming the political leadership of Connecticut. Led by the Wolcotts, "Pope" Timothy Dwight, and the *Courant,* they exhibited a dual reaction from the moderate liberal nationalism of Federalism's early years. The Union was still new. It had yet to attach to itself the passionate popular nationalism that subsequent history would create. Such leaders of the upper rank as Wadsworth and Wolcott Jr. had regarded the Federal Union with reservations, as desirable but not necessarily permanent. Now they developed a conservative sectionalism defined in New England terms, which they invoked to rally support for the Administration in Congress and for their leadership in the state.

Believing in their region's superiority in statecraft, economy, culture, and institutions, they sought to enhance the New England influence nationally so as to defeat the Gallophiles, prevent the South from gaining control at Philadelphia, and preserve civilization as they understood it to be. Already some were holding in reserve Rufus King's alternative of a Northern confederacy or nation while they continued in alliance with the Southern Federalists under Hamilton's political leadership, satisfied with this as long as it facilitated the adoption of policies favorable to the New England economy and institutional life.

The intense anti-Southern prejudice that was expressed by the Connecticut Wits between 1788 and 1797 was a reaction to the bitter intersectional struggle for power in the federal government. Dr. Hopkins expressed this repeatedly in letters to Wolcott Jr. before publishing "Guillotina" in the *Courant.* Anti-Southernism spread to the political essays published in that journalistic leader of Connecticut opinion in 1796. As phrased there, that viewpoint voiced a growing awareness of cultural differences with the South, enhanced as they were by gradual emancipation in New England and Pennsylvania while slavery was expanding south of the Potomac. Emerging free society in the Northern states, vigorous, experiencing the confident impulse of neutral trade, sparkling and satirical in its literary articulation, was challenging the South with adverse value judgments that extended from slavery and the plantation system to education and morals.[1]

As long as General Washington was President, his personal ascendancy restrained the interregional struggle for power, while his reliance upon Hamilton's advice on questions of high policy gave Federalist nationalism a continuing impetus. However, Hamilton had left the Treasury. Wolcott Jr. agreed with Webster and Dr. Hopkins that national well-being depended upon New England's dominance in the United States, a sectional viewpoint that contrasted none too subtly with the Hamiltonian nationalism to which the new Secretary of the Treasury paid lip service. Hamilton, it should be recalled, was a West Indian, appreciative of the plantation mind's potential nationalism, which he cultivated among the commercial planters of Virginia and South Carolina while developing a polity advantageous to all parts of the commercial economy of the seaboard.

The Wolcott faction was beginning to forget that the Virginia and South Carolina statesman had played a most important role in fashioning the Federal Union (in what appears to have been a deliberate attempt to frustrate the Northern separatism of 1785–1786), in which their regional interests might find protection and satisfaction. Although some of these figures had deserted the Federalists for Jefferson's party, others remained loyal to Washington. The major political problem confronting the Federalists, in view of the Republicans' great strength in the South, was how to preserve and strengthen their Southern wing, since only four Congressmen from that region had voted to carry Jay's Treaty into effect. As Hamilton understood, this could be achieved only by a national policy whereby high offices and power were shared interregionally. And yet, in March 1796, acting Governor Oliver Wolcott Sr. of Connecticut informed his son in the Treasury Department of his agreement with Webster's forecast of an inevitable separation of North and South as a result of their different interests and political views! [2]

The rapport between Northern and Southern Federalists was being weakened by the New England group's growing hostility to French principles and example, which were especially popular in the South; by its fear of an apparently destructive "Democracy" whose appeal to the urban populace produced turbulence; and by antipathy to religious "Infidelity," whether the deism of Paine and Voltaire or the atheism of Baron d'Holbach that had assisted the French Revolution's disestablishment of the Church and the overthrow of the monarchy and aristocracy. To the admirers of "Pope" Dwight of Yale College, "Jacobinism" was as destructive of religion as it was of society and civilization.[3] The greater strength of Francophile Republicanism in the South and Jefferson's increasingly formidable bid for national power frightened the Yale-Litchfield men with the hydra-headed specter of lost political leadership, the subordination of their region and state to the plantation South, and the possibility of a revolutionary upheaval destructive of their way of life.

The open attempts of the French Minister, Pierre Auguste Adet, to kill Jay's Treaty during 1795–1796 [4] evinced to the Wolcotts and their following the continuation of revolutionary France's intention to displace the Federalists and elevate the pro-French party to power. To alert Federalists, Adet's activity was not only an infringement upon American sovereignty. It presaged also the attempt to establish in the United States a puppet regime actively allied with but subordinate to France.[5] This stimulated a nationalist reaction in the Federalist Party that was at variance with developing New England sectionalism, thus strengthening a dualism that had characterized that party from its foundation.

There was danger that the Wolcott leadership might destroy Federalism as a national political movement and place sectionalism in the ascendant in American life, either within the Federal Union or in the form of regional governments.

Actually, Hamiltonian nationalism as a system of policy and ideas was considerably in advance of actualities. Methods of travel and transportation were such that they delayed the arrival in the capital of Congressmen and Senators for weeks beyond Congress' opening date. Each district, state, and larger region lived in a condition of semi-isolation,[6] which only merchants, navigators, speculators, wealthy landowners, lawyers, and clergy transcended in their travels, dealings, and reading. The press' emphasis upon European and national news also tended to counteract the prevailing provincialism of American life. This was so strong, however, as to present to public men an alternative basis for government and politics. It was the experience of the War of Independence and the renewed dangers explicit in the War of the French Revolution which made the national approach to American problems pre-eminently practical as *the* means of fostering American interests and preserving independence for all but the most provincial and embittered.[7]

The weakness of popular nationalism in the presence of existing provincialism, the precarious foreign situation, and the bitterness of major interregional rivalries at the capital were related to the demand during the spring of 1796 that Washington accept election for a third term. The bitter attacks on him by the partisans of the Franco-American alliance which Jay's Treaty had undermined, while leading to his decision to retire from public life in disgust,[8] appeared to men like the Wolcotts to document the threat that the

Gallophiles presented to American independence and Northern interests.[9]

During the bitter partisan struggle precipitated by Washington's Farewell Address three months before the meeting of the Presidential electors in December, the Federalists identified their cause with patriotism, assailed French political intrigues, defended Jay's Treaty as creating *"an alliance of interest"* with Great Britain, and attacked the Franco-American alliance. Jefferson's personal popularity, traditional attachment to that alliance, and hostility to Jay's Treaty made the contest doubtful. Adet's open support of Jefferson's candidacy, his notes to Secretary of State Timothy Pickering demanding abrogation of Jay's Treaty and a revival of the Franco-American alliance, and his suspension of his diplomatic status so as to enable him to aid the Republican Party on the eve of the election, played into Federalist hands.[10]

However, the Federalists divided into hostile factions in the face of the Franco-Republican challenge. Hamilton urged loyal support of the intersectional Presidential ticket composed of John Adams and Thomas Pinckney, a South Carolina Federalist diplomat recently returned from Madrid. Because of Adams' weakness in the South, consistent adherence to this policy by the Northern Federalists would have ensured Pinckney's election. This, to Hamilton, seemed to be the best method of perpetuating his national financial system. Adams' friends sought actively to elevate him to the Presidency and were attacked vigorously by the more ardent Hamiltonians.

Although he was Hamilton's friend and professed supporter, Wolcott Jr. viewed Pinckney's candidacy with misgivings. To Governor Wolcott Sr. it was entirely unpalatable. They worked to secure Adams' election. Governor Wolcott urged privately upon his son the alternative of Northern secession from the Union should either Pinckney or Jefferson be elected President. A follower of his, the essayist "Pelham" in the *Courant,* urged this upon the public.

Both the Governor and "Pelham" maintained that only separation from the South in such a contingency could safeguard Northern institutions and interests.[11]

Paralleling this, in late November and early December Wolcott Jr. supplied his father, the Essex Junto, and prominent Federalists in other Northern states with copies of French Minister Adet's notes to Pickering. These he accompanied with indignant comments upon this "insulting" French infringement of American independence and with campaign information indicating Pinckney's election if all Northern Federalist electors supported him and Adams equally. Although he recommended this course formally, he also intimated that the Federalist leaders in each state should exercise their best judgment. They did so on December 7 in a manner designed to ensure Adams' election instead.[12]

This leadership defeated Hamilton's tactic, to which only the most ardent Northern Hamiltonians adhered. At Hartford, when the Connecticut Presidential electors met, they decided—including Wadsworth and Elias Perkins—to vote solidly for Adams while diverting five of their nine second ballots from Pinckney to the Chief Justice. In Massachusetts Wolcott Jr.'s friends diverted a similar though not proportionate portion of their second votes from the South Carolinian. In the Northern states a total of eighteen electoral votes were withheld from him in this manner, more than enough to defeat South Carolina's similar but reverse tactic. That the Northern electors' desertion of Pinckney (and Hamilton) was attributable in a considerable measure to the Wolcotts' appeal to sectionalism and Gallophobia is indubitable.[13]

Coit was in Philadelphia attending the final session of the Fourth Congress when the Wolcotts made their extraordinary coup after publicly offering, via "Pelham," Northern secession as the alternative to victory. Elias Perkins informed him of the proceedings and action of the Connecticut presidential electors promptly. Sore though Coit may have been at having been passed over twice for the United

States Senate in behalf of Wolcott adherents, he approved of the diversion of five of the second ballots from Pinckney. In reply to Perkins, he remarked that "throwing away of votes in Connecticut" was "well judged—the people in Massachusetts have played their game, I think, not so judiciously as you did. 'tis still (from the information we have) or rather *has been* in the power of S Carolina to give Mr. P the Vice Presidency by throwing away their votes from Mr. J. This is the only circumstance at present deemed doubtful." He predicted confidently on December 17 Adams' election by a margin of three electoral votes over Jefferson, two weeks before this result was announced unofficially.[14]

On Christmas Day he forwarded corroborative data, adding:

> We have nothing new—our Democrats have talked of their apprehensions of a French War till I believe they are almost tired of it. We have nothing on that subject since I wrote you, our business has hardly got going yet. While Reports are printing & our Committees in Consideration we have little to do in the House.[15]

Coit's reaction to the Wolcott coup which ensured the inclusion of Secretary of the Treasury Wolcott Jr. in Adams' Cabinet was typical of the New England Federalists. However, he evinced more than a narrowing sectionalism when in the Committee of the Whole he voted with Griswold for direct taxes *except on slaves*. The pair and the moderates voted with the Republicans to suspend manning the three frigates of the new navy, a project dear to Wolcott Jr. and to Hamilton. This was rebellion by two Congressmen from the Thames Valley against the Litchfield leadership of the Wolcotts, either because the farmers of eastern Connecticut disliked higher taxes to finance the frigates or because of the land speculation scandal of 1795 and the new contingent secessionism that tainted the Wolcott faction in Connecticut.

Then, ostensibly in behalf of greater customs efficiency, Coit persuaded the House to ask Wolcott Jr. to prepare for it "a system for comprising into one the various laws now in being for laying and collecting duties on imports and tonnage, and for reducing to specific rates of duty, articles which had heretofore been charged according to value." This request anticipated the nineteenth-century maxim that specific duties were preferable to ad valorem ones because they reduced temptations at the customs house and were fairer. Possibly Coit had learned of serious customs losses being incurred by the Treasury because of the derelictions of its agents—which Wolcott Jr. would admit privately a year later. In mid-February 1797 Coit assured Colonel Wadsworth that definitive action on "Direct & indirect taxes" was unlikely and that the predictions of an embargo were unfounded.[16]

Coit returned to Philadelphia for the special session of the Fifth Congress that President Adams called to meet on May 15 after learning that France had rejected the American Minister, General Charles Cotesworth Pinckney, while despoiling American shipping in retaliation for Jay's Treaty. The United States was on the verge of war with the French Republic. Congress met three days after Governor-elect Wolcott Sr. asked the Connecticut legislature to protect the state from "unprovoked" French "aggressions" and "evils of still greater magnitude which this conduct is probably intended to produce." In the House at Philadelphia, Coit headed the Committee on Elections and secured appointment of a "Standing Committee on Revised and Unfinished Business."

He alienated many Federalists, however, when he and Speaker Dayton attempted to keep the door open to further negotiation with the French Republic by securing a softening of the asperity of those sections of the House's draft "Address" to the President that referred to France's rejection of Pinckney as the American Minister. An inaccurate report of Coit's share of this maneuver in the *Connecticut Courant,* attributable probably to Goodrich, led to criticism of this action in Connecticut.[17] There, the secessionist political essayist "Gustavus," professedly but not necessarily a resident of

New London County, attempted to inflame the state by asking if France was not attempting to precipitate civil war in the United States "and finally eradicate our federal constitution?" Could Republicans "claim of being friends to their country?" Yet, although his followers had opened fire on Coit, Governor Wolcott informed Hamilton that neither he "or any of the public officers" were "desirous of producing a War with France." [18]

Secretary Wolcott Jr. informed George Cabot almost simultaneously that the United States "must prepare for a serious state of things" that would continue "for a considerable time & to meet which firmness, decision & system are indispensible." What was needed were armaments to defend commerce, including "Ships of War" for convoying, the fortification of ports, new revenues, and negotiation by "a minister as near the Directory as he shall be suffered, to improve any opportunity for . . . amicable adjustment, but never to disgrace our Government." [19]

The Adams policy developed this further. It comprised continued non-involvement in the European conflict, strengthened armaments, and further negotiations with France. The President then appointed the famous three-man special mission to France. It was composed of General C. C. Pinckney, the rejected diplomat; John Marshall of Virginia; and Elbridge Gerry of Massachusetts.

Partisan passions were greatly inflamed, however, by the repeated publication in the Federalist press immediately before Congress convened, and for months thereafter, of an authentic translation of a letter from Thomas Jefferson to Philip Mazzei, dated April 24, 1796. This was taken from the French translation that had appeared recently in the official *Le Moniteur* in Paris in an attempt to discredit the Federalist Party and to demonstrate that the Republicans in the United States were favorable to France. In this extraordinary missive Jefferson castigated Washington's leadership. He described the Federalists as renegade American patriots who had degenerated into "an Anglican monarchical aristocratical party," and their leaders as former "Samsons" and "Solomons . . . shorn by the harlot England." [20] The resentment in Connecticut at Coit's amendment of the House "Address" so as to facilitate the new negotiation with France was undoubtedly related to the indignation provoked by the letter to Mazzei.

A hardening intolerance of political differences was developing among the Federalists. This had been presaged by the Wolcotts' antipathy to France, French doctrines, and the South. Further independence in Congress on Coit's part was certain to invite serious criticism from the Federalist leaders.

Adams' defense policy, which demanded enlargement of the navy for use in commerce protection and modest increase of the army, contrasted with Hamilton's desire for a more ambitious program including a federal militia. This situation gave Coit an opportunity to act independently, with its inevitable consequences.

Although the New England Federalists were aggressive Northern sectionalists, they favored the navy and a standing army as nationalizing measures. However, the commercial farming districts' support was essential for this and for continued Federalist dominance nationally. These, like the remote self-sufficient farming areas, were reluctant to bear the increased taxes to finance heavier armaments. Among the Connecticut Congressmen Coit was especially sensitive to the farmers' viewpoint, not only because he was a would-be farm owner but also because he came from a region of mixed commercial and self-sufficient farming, whose pockets of rich earth were interspersed between wide areas of thin and rocky soils. New London and Norwich were the outlets for agricultural eastern Connecticut. Coit's thrifty attitude toward the new frigates was understandable.

He desired, obviously, to retain in the Federalist Party the moderates from similar mixed or strictly commercial farming areas, whom the Republicans were courting assiduously as the landowners' party in an astute bid for control of the balance of national and intrastate power. In no Northern state, it must be recalled, were the commercial, maritime, and industrial elements sufficiently strong numerically to carry elections by their votes alone. Victory for either major party depended upon the political alignment of the commercial farmers. Thus Coit's reaction to the rival Adams and Hamilton programs was governed by more than pique, frustrated ambition, or power rivalry with the Wolcott coterie.[21]

During the special session, Coit adhered neither to it nor to the Hamilton policy which that element supported, but mainly to the bipartisan moderates in the House, whose fourteen votes held the balance between the rival parties. This middle group refused to commit itself unqualifiedly to "strong measures," in part because of trade stagnation and numerous bankruptcies. The situation resulting from the much resented French spoliations diminished the public's ability to bear heavier taxes. However, Adams' special mission to Paris was generally approved of as a means of avoiding war.

Coit's action on individual measures illuminated his position, which was not entirely consistent. He and Speaker Dayton so amended the bill for arming merchant vessels, which Adams and Hamilton desired, as to defeat its object and lead the sponsors to join the Republicans in rejecting the modified bill. Backed by Griswold, Coit cast his vote against coast-defense galleys, which the rough North Atlantic waters would have made almost useless. He opposed using revenue cutters to protect shipping, possibly because of their light armament. Then he led the extreme Federalists, including Samuel Sewall, in emasculating an extradition bill, although the moderates favored it because it rejected Britain's doctrine of inalienable allegiance. With Griswold and Goodrich, he voted for the bill's postponement. After that he rejoined the moderates, who sided with the Republicans in defeating the additional artillery regiment bill. Coit even voted against an increased appropriation for coast defense, while urging his wife again to agree to remove to a farm for greater safety.

His negative vote was decisive in defeating the bill to authorize use of the navy in convoying. He voted with a large majority to strike nine twenty-gun sloops from the naval program.[22] Since he had voted originally for the frigates that would form the backbone of the new navy, Coit was obviously motivated in this opposition to a larger fleet and convoying by more than thrift and antipathy to the Wolcotts.

On the same day as the reduction of the naval program, he demanded successfully that the naval bill be limited to a single year. His vote was decisive in establishing the principle of annual appropriations for the navy, against the opposition of the other Connecticut members and most Federalists who wished for a long-term commitment. Without citing the established precedent of annual appropriations for the army, he declared:

> For his part he did not wish a permanent naval establishment in this country. He would rather see the frigates at the wharves than see them go out to sea. He trusted a majority of the House would one day be of his opinion, and, if such a change of sentiment should take place, he wished to put it in their power to annul the establishment.[23]

This little-America position, assumed despite the virtual defenselessness of the large American neutral trade, the belligerents' humiliating depredations upon it, and continued British impressments, approached the viewpoint of the agrarian Republicans. It was far removed from orthodox New England Federalism and even more so from Hamilton's demand for naval power adequate to defend commerce and strengthen the diplomatic hand of the United States.

The debate on this navy bill was significant for another reason. Immediately before the final vote on it on June 24, Samuel Sewall's bitterness at the Southern Republicans' opposition boiled over. As if he were voicing the secessionist sentiment that the Wolcott following must have discussed repeatedly in the corridors and committee rooms, he declared that since the representatives of "the agricultural interests" lacked knowledge of how to protect commerce "they had better suffer the country to be divided." Apparently the contingent secessionists were the most ardent advocates of a large navy.

Nathaniel Macon of North Carolina countered with cool surprise. He suggested that if Sewall was serious and thought that it would benefit his constituents, he should "bring forward a motion to divide the Union." After Speaker Dayton called them both to order, Albert Gallatin asserted that he favored assisting agriculture and commerce, but he was opposed to the navy bill because it was "totally inadequate to its object." This was insincere. He and his following had aided the moderates in reducing its authorizations.

Coit then voted with Gallatin and the Republican die-hards in a vain, last-minute attempt to defeat the bill's provision for completion of three frigates and the construction of a few twenty-gun sloops of war. These were built in time to go to sea during the X Y Z crisis of the following spring.[24] If one thing was clear from this situation, it was that Coit was not a Northern secessionist. He survived to vote for the navy at the next session with moderation. Obviously he did not share the Wolcotts' and Ellsworth's admiration for Rufus King.

Coit's opposition to convoying remained unexplained. This may be attributed to his non-involvement position, since convoying could have led to war with France.

Temporarily, Coit had passed from a thrifty insistence upon a navy that commercial agriculture could afford (in opposition to excessive armaments that would lead to political disaster, such as the Federalists would experience when they lost control of Congress and the Presidency in 1800)[25] to an inexplicable opposition to a permanent navy. As a Federalist moderate, he was almost alone in voting with the Republicans against the navy bill in opposition to the immediate interests of his city, state, and region. The other moderates joined the extreme Federalists in enacting it. This action made Coit vulnerable to attack on the ground of disloyalty to his party and region.

Two days after passage of the navy bill, Secretary Wolcott Jr. intimated to him that an explanation should be forthcoming, probably when they met at a social function. In reply, Coit described "some Circumstances" that had lessened him in the Cabinet member's "Estimation." Afterward, in the evening, Coit elaborated upon his remarks in a long letter to the Secretary. He described himself as an independent moderate anxious to avoid "improvident Expenditures" which might "bring on premature old age and decrepitude on the Finances of the Country." The "chances of security to be derived from the Expenditures of a Navey against which I have voted, have not been worth those expenditures," a realistic statement in view of the overwhelming superiority of the British and French fleets compared with the slender navy that Congress had voted. If, in making this "estimate I may have erred of the principle & motives of my actions I cannot fail to be perfectly assured & satisfied." This he added in calm defiance that may have implied another, more fundamental consideration.

He then tendered a psychological explanation of his position:

> Constitutionally inclined to moderation—not capable of feeling the warmth which appears to me to have existed in the parties which have agitated our public Councils since I have been among them, & not perfectly approving at all times the measures pursued by either, I have wished for some middle station on which a man might place himself—the difficulty of finding such a station where it is a question if it exists—the difficulty of forming one unless a man possessed more talents than I do, & the unpleasantness of fluctuating from one party to another—I need not explain to you; yet in my situation, little conscious of talents, & valuing no consideration superior to my own estimation for integrity, what could I do. *I could find no path to satisfy myself in but to form my judgment on the best information*

I could get, and to act on each individual measure as appeared to me right—if in attempting to pursue this path personal prejudices, or other similar Considerations have biased my judgment; it would not I confess be extraordinary, but I can truly declare that if such has been the case, it has been insensibly to myself & against my wishes.

Disclaiming fear of "executive influence" in the House, lest he appear to resent Wolcott's interest in his course, and uncritical of administrative inefficiency, he attributed his thrifty statesmanship in part to his moderate means. This was a double dig at Wolcott Jr.'s attempt to determine the policies to be supported by the Connecticut members and at the wealth which he displayed. Although his father had been a moderately wealthy merchant, Coit said:

> My habits having been formed in a situation almost below mediocrity in point of property, it is very probable that my Ideas of Economy in the scale of public Expenditure may in some instances approach to parsimony, but so strong is the passion of national pride, & so fascinating are the arguments addressed to the passions by Considerations of splendor, magnificence dignity & generosity that I cannot but be persuaded that the general Biass is the other way.

He concluded by advising Wolcott Jr. on how Cabinet members might more effectively inform the House of departmental needs. The legislators' "Confidence" in the executive, he observed, depended upon a "liberal" supply of "Information," as if he were anticipating the viewpoint of Congressmen ever since.[26]

For an admirer of Hamilton, Coit exhibited a unique method of expressing his opposition to the Wolcotts' leadership.

That very day, Coit had expressed misgivings regarding the proposed stamp tax when discussing the revenue bill in the House. During its subsequent consideration, he was outvoted in his attempt to prevent a graduated tax on debentures. He defeated Gallatin's amendment to levy the stamp tax on vellum only at the capital, blocked the attempt to levy it on playing cards, and helped to prevent its extension to military land patents, which were held largely by speculators and intending settlers. These actions evinced a realistic appreciation of the popular dislike of such a tax, as well as of its relation to the profit position of speculators and bankers. The latter he assisted by preventing extension of that tax to bank notes. He voted with his party to impose licenses on retailers of imported liquors. He failed to secure a 50 per cent drawback on the imported salt duty for the fisheries, but accepted 33⅓ per cent, which was all the moderates and Republicans would allow New England in retaliation for the heavier imposts levied on farmers and consumers. He voted for the amended bill.[27]

His return to an approximation of party regularity did not save him from the wrath of the Wolcott faction and Essex Junto. On July 10 the *Connecticut Courant* reprinted damaging praise of his vote against the navy bill that "Middlesex" had contributed to the Republican *Boston Chronicle*. The *Courant's* editors, Hudson and Goodwin, who also published Noah Webster's *Spelling Book* and *Grammatical Institutes,* predicted bitterly the termination of Coit's political career in less than two years after he had completed "his voyage" to Republicanism. Simultaneously, in the *Courant,* "Gustavus" impugned Coit's fitness to represent Connecticut in Congress because of his opposition to "efficient measures for the security of our country" and his veering "over to the Anti-federal side of politics." Coming as it did from the aged secessionist spokesman, this was not especially damaging. However, *The Weekly Oracle's* republication in New London of the "Middlesex" piece without comment two days later brought the issue home to eastern Connecticut.

On the other hand, Coit's regularity during consideration of the revenue bill won praise from the Federalist *Columbian Centinel* of Boston. So did the card that he inserted in the *Chronicle* to correct its misinterpretation of his "character and principles" and to request that it publish no further eulogia of himself.[28] His rebellion from the Wolcott leadership was strictly intraparty. Scrutiny of Congressional proceedings during the special session discloses that he was a most influential leader of the bipartisan moderates. However, he achieved this position at the expense of the leadership that he had exercised hitherto in the Connecticut delegation.

In eastern Connecticut, his course attracted sufficient support to promise a profitable clientele to Charles Holt, who founded the aggressive, Republican *Bee* in New London that summer. Holt quickly repudiated "Gustavus," terming grossly unfair his repeated attacks on the South. Holt ridiculed "Gustavus'" invitation to the South to "secede" so as to enable the North to perpetuate for itself alone the advantages of federal union under the Constitution of 1787.[29] After the appearance of such an aggressive opposition paper in his own city in rivalry with the *Gazette* and *Weekly Oracle,* Coit found himself between two political fires.

However, his letters to Bob that spring from Philadelphia exhibited no evidence of strain. Proud of his nine-year-old son's cleverness at school, he asked him, "Have you begun your Greek & how do you like it?" before quizzing him about his garden and the tending of "the old Cow." As for "the Rice, I hope that comes on cleverly, and should like very well to get enough for one pudding out of our own Garden," he added in mid-June.[30]

With such imperturbability, Coit returned to New London after Congress adjourned, to confront the increasing coolness of his clients and those Union Bank associates who preferred the stronger Wolcott line in national policy. However, without dignifying the issue unnecesarily by washing dirty party linen in public, he had made clear to the Wolcotts and their following his unflinching opposition to the contingent secession policy by resisting their preferred armament policies, which endangered the public credit but which were necessary for national defense and foreign policy. Although he came from New London, whose Nathan Hale, a Yale

College alumnus, had given to Americans in 1776 the conception of "my country," Coit had allowed his frustrated ambition and opposition to the Wolcotts to push him into political revolt against a naval policy that he had originally supported.

CHAPTER SEVEN

Prelude to ℭ*risis*

WHEN the Fifth Congress reconvened in November 1797, President Adams reiterated his demand for a defense program to strengthen the position of the special mission to France. Moderate armaments, he maintained, would benefit all occupations. The cost should be financed from new taxes because of the burden of the public debt. The financial situation led the moderates of the House to examine each proposed measure carefully. While awaiting news of the negotiation in Paris, however, the division of Congress into the "High" Federalists, who sought national strength to enhance American prestige and trade,[1] the bipartisan moderates, and the orthodox Republicans, made it impossible to secure action upon the Administration program. Its supporters, perforce, had to delay until they heard from the special mission at Paris.

Coit was again Chairman of the Committee of Elections. He undoubtedly enjoyed his association with Samuel Sewall, his former Harvard classmate and fellow member of the Speaking Club, and with Griswold and Nathaniel Smith of Connecticut. Calm moderate that he was, Coit was probably irritated by the choleric intolerance of Republicanism exhibited by the tall freshman member of the Connecticut delegation, John ("The Goth") Allen, a new member of the Yale-Litchfield element who became the bellwether of the High Federalists. Chauncey Goodrich's cold indifference and the anonymous hostility of the "Congressional Proceedings" that he probably contributed to the *Courant* indicated to Coit the Wolcott faction's attitude toward him.[2]

During those months of waiting, the House debates became increasingly acrimonious. Gallatin accused the High Federalists of attempting to provoke war with France. He appealed to the moderates to force a change in the Adams policy. During bitter exchanges, the Republicans also accused the President of leading a political party and of confining the patronage to its members. Griswold replied that this should be the practice but the President did not follow it consistently. Sewall conceded grudgingly that "the opposition had the right to exist." These statements were significant departures from the customary assertions by members of all shades of belief that they were guided by their independent judgment and by considerations of national welfare rather than by party. This had been Washington's official position. "Faction" was still viewed with distrust, after the fashion set by *The Federalist*. However, a clearer understanding of the character and function of political parties was crystallizing amid the prolonged partisan struggle.[3]

Coit labored in Congress under the psychological disadvantage of his wife's enhanced opposition to his long absences from home. After his return to Philadelphia, she discovered herself pregnant with their sixth child. Depressed, she wrote him on February 4, 1798, demanding bluntly to be informed when he intended to resign. Affectionately and most sympathetically, he replied that he wished that he could inform her when he proposed "quitting the line of Life which separates me so much from you. I wish to do it most sincerely. I am tired of it for my own sake and my Family's."

As for what he would do after retirement from Congress, he observed that he did not "think of returning to seek for Business at the Bar—my former success there combined with a variety of Considerations made it no pleasant Situation to me. . . . 'Tis in a degree uncertain how I might succeed on returning. . . . I must follow some Business. Have patience, my dear Nancy, and hope with me that it will not be a great while before something more favourable to your wishes and mine will turn up. I am afflicted with the peculiarly unpleasant situation in which I leave you this winter."[4]

He continued in Congress in his role of the efficient, working Congressman, calm, speaking only when necessary, conciliatory. He secured a select committee that prepared a bill to improve the patent law and then secured its passage.[5] Despite the reiterated protest of Matthew Lyon of Vermont, he supported continuance of the House's custom of presenting en masse its formal "Address" to the President in reply to his annual speech to Congress. Coit seconded Robert Goodloe Harper's successful motion for a select committee to prepare a federal bankruptcy bill. He was second on this committee, its work stimulated by Robert Morris' spectacular bankruptcy and fall from eminence. Meanwhile, Coit voted hesitantly to instruct the committee on the President's speech to bring in a bill to facilitate national defense and the protection of trade. He opposed Gallatin's attempt to enforce the federal statute of limitations on certain claims. He insisted successfully, when Harper presented a bankruptcy bill of his own devising, that all chairmen make reports that contained their respective committees' decisions rather than their individual views.[6]

Thriftily, Coit sought "official information" on the location of the boundary of the Indian lands in Tennessee before voting compensation to settlers displaced there by the recent treaty. Yet, contrary to the usual practice, he supported Harper's bill to appropriate funds in anticipation of additional claims from sufferers from British seizures of vessels in American waters. The impartial observer might have wondered if the variance in the New Londoner's position stemmed from the different partisan affiliations of the sufferers in these cases.[7]

While thus disclosing that he was influenced by rising partisanship in Congress, Coit was encouraged when the Connecticut freemen ranked him second on the list of seventeen Congressional nominees.[8] The Wolcott faction's attacks on him had not yet undermined his popularity. He studiously avoided personalities in debate, possibly to avoid embittering further the tense situation.

He may have realized that inauguration of President Timothy Dwight's counterattack upon "Infidel Philosophy" at the Yale College Commencement, September 9, presaged a profound change in the socio-political psychology of Connecticut. As this developed, it would intensify the reaction of Federalism away from its moderate liberalism of the mid-eighties and inevitably impair his political position as a liberal Federalist.[9]

On January 30, when outside the bar, he was startled and outraged when he was told that Matthew Lyon had just spit in Roger Griswold's face before the fireplace of the House. A few minutes earlier, he had passed Speaker Dayton and Lyon there when he left the floor, as the Vermonter said loudly that the Connecticut members did not represent their constituents and impugned their integrity and public spirit. After Coit left, Lyon had threatened to establish a Republican paper and precipitate a political revolution in Connecticut. Upon hearing that, Griswold, who sat nearby, approached him and smilingly suggested that if he wished to accomplish this objective he should wear his "wooden sword." This stinging reference to Lyon's (probably unjust) cashiering as a militia subaltern in 1776 so inflamed him that he turned and spat in Griswold's face in retaliation. He had declared upon entering Congress that he would know how to resent such an insult. Although tempted to take summary vengeance for the retaliatory insult to himself, Griswold was restrained by respect for the House and then by his fellow members.

Indignant, already disgusted at Lyon's previous crude behavior, the Federalists secured an investigation by a strict party vote with a view to his expulsion. To prevent a duel in the interim, the House ruled that it would be "a high breach of privilege" if either man "shall enter into a personal contest until the house shall be heard thereon."

The Committee of Privileges took voluminous testimony, including Lyon's "Narrative" of his cashiering, subsequent service as a captain in the Continental Army during the Saratoga campaign under General St. Clair, and his public career in Vermont. Coit informed the Committee that he had paid little attention to the Lyon-Dayton conversation preliminary to his departure from the floor. After hearing eyewitness testimony, the Committee recommended Lyon's expulsion for his "violent attack and gross indecency, committed on the person of Roger Griswold."

Lyon then presented a prepared defense in the House, asserting that he was "incapable of an intentional violation" of its rules. In doing so, however, he extemporized in such indecent language that he shocked the members and the gallery again. After claiming that Coit had been rude to him during the hearing, he justified his own earlier castigation of the Connecticut delegation by bitter reference to "the kind of politeness" that its members "make use of towards their opponents" before he spoke indecently of a Vermont opponent.

An amendment was immediately moved to include in the motion for expulsion the phrase "for a gross indecency of language in his defence before the house." While the members expressed their indignation at Lyon's second breach of Congressional propriety, Coit arose and attempted to persuade the members to restrict the grounds for expulsion to the first episode. It was possible, he observed, that the indecency might have been uttered "inadvertantly," and in any case the House should not dignify it. As for himself, he held Lyon in contempt and would vote for his expulsion. Although this intervention was motivated undoubtedly by the calm sense of propriety and proportion that distinguished Coit's attitude toward public questions, it proved to be very costly to him politically.

Privately, he informed his wife that Lyon was "a vile infamous Fellow," and that he hoped for his expulsion by the necessary two-thirds majority.

So great was the House's indignation at the Vermonter's indecent language that Coit's intervention was futile. Speaker Dayton, with whom he had been on cordial terms, declared hotly that Coit had become Lyon's defender by sanctioning in this manner, supposedly, his "plea" that "he did not know he was violating the rules of the house—*he did it through inadvertence!*" Dayton insisted upon the amendment, which was adopted.

Coit closed the Committee of the Whole's debate on the amended motion to expel, arguing dispassionately against Republican technicalities. He maintained that the House's constitutional power to expel must be invoked against "a man who would produce nothing but disorder and confusion in their proceedings" and had committed a "brutal, indecent and unmannerly" act. He voted with the majority of fifty-two to expel. This was somewhat less than the required two-thirds because the Republicans, although disgusted with Lyon, voted in the negative so as to retain his vote.[10]

"Decus" in Fenno's Federalist *Gazette of the United States* then denounced Coit unfairly as "the most extravagant advocate for Lyon" because of his attempt to restrict the case against him for expulsion to the original act. Fenno added sarcastically, "Mr. Coit is probably ambitious to deserve and receive another applauding and congratulatory address from the democratic papers, on his return" home, a biting allusion to the *Boston Chronicle's* praise of him the previous July.

Although he probably attributed this assault to personal animus and extreme partisanship, Coit was fortunate that Fenno did not award him editorially a charter membership in the *"Knights of the Wooden Sword."* Coit was aware undoubtedly that Fenno depended upon Secretary of the Treasury Wolcott Jr.'s patronage. Almost immediately after "Decus'" piece appeared in the *Gazette,* Coit was informed reliably that it had been written by Theodore Sedgwick, High Federalist Massachusetts Senator of the Essex Junto. Coit promptly addressed him in a dignified, sarcastic, unsigned note, asking if he was the author:

Will Mr. Sedgwick pardon Mr Coit for asking him if he is the
Author of a piece in Fenno's Paper this Evening under the signature
of Decus?—

The Question Mr. C. is aware ought to be accompanied with an
Apology—as his Apology Mr. C. takes the liberty of mentioning the
Freedom with which Mr. S. has heretofore permitted Mr. C. to ad-
dress him—to this he will only add for his own justification (not that
he has the vanity to suppose the Information of any Importance to
Mr. S.) that the piece alluded to has excited in his mind no single
Sentiment of Anger or Resentment. Sentiments of mortification, but
not for himself it has excited.

Phila. 11 Feby 1798

No record of Sedgwick's answer survives. Mortified by the public
ventilation of factionalism within their party, Coit exhibited poise
and maturity in replying to that bitter attack in this manner. His
self-possession explains his continuing influence as a moderate as the
struggle between the moderates and extremists continued.

He understood the damage done to him in Connecticut when the
Courant republished "Decus'" diatribe. However, "Plain Truth"
from Philadelphia defended him in that paper with a discriminating
account of his actual course during the episode, observing that "in a
high degree" he "possesses, and deserves" the "confidence" of "his
constituents," and that Lyon's indecent language should not have
been "put in competition with his insult to Mr. Griswold," as Coit
had insisted. The public believed generally that the House had made
"a political question" of the matter.[11]

However, the Federalist social world held that Griswold had to
"beat" Lyon "either in or out of the House," and that Federalism
had to have "a champion" since expulsion of Lyon had failed. After
leading Federalists demanded that he wreak vengeance upon
Lyon,[12] Griswold attacked him on the floor of the House on the
morning of February 15 immediately before the Speaker was to

resume his chair. After Griswold struck Lyon with a heavy walking stick as he rose from his desk, the latter seized the fire tongs and replied in kind. They clinched, fell, rolled on the floor, and Griswold gained the upper hand before the members separated them, only to have them attempt to renew the combat outside the bar. Later, "at the watering place," Lyon attacked Griswold in retaliation. This unprecedented brawl aroused popular disgust and ridicule. Yet the House's earlier ruling had conceded to Griswold a right to seek satisfaction after expulsion of Lyon was rejected. No Federalist had anticipated, however, that Lyon would prove to be so tough a nut to crack.

The Congressmen were stung by this violent scene. It was far less dignified than a formal duel would have been, although the latter was prohibited by the rules. In the members' hearing on Philadelphia streets, citizens were observing ironically to each other, "You need not go to the house to day, there is no business to do there, as there is no fighting there to day."

The Committee of Privileges investigated further and reported negatively on the motion to expel. Coit voted with the majority to uphold the report. The House then ordered that both men pledge themselves not to commit any further acts of violence upon each other during the session, on penalty of imprisonment by the sergeant at arms until they so promised. Coit cast the deciding vote against Robert Williams' motion to instruct the Speaker also to reprimand both men formally, which would have been almost equivalent to a request for their resignations. Speaker Dayton called Griswold and Lyon to the rostrum and read them the House's order. They made the required pledge.[13]

The House's mild reproof for that extraordinary breach of its dignity and rules must be ascribed to the intense partisanship that made each party anxious to prevent the discipline of a member, and also to a lingering respect for the prohibited code duello. Today, both men would be expelled instantly for such actions as they indulged in early in 1798 on the floor of the House.

Although the Republicans prevented Lyon's expulsion, they condemned his method and the place that he selected for showing his resentment of Griswold's "wooden sword" insult with its direct allusion to the blunt weapon that had been fastened to the Vermonter's belt when he was cashiered in 1776. Madison wrote to Jefferson that a duel between them later would have been preferable to the "tedious & disgraceful debates in Congress" that the episode precipitated. While reprobating Lyon's violation of the dignity of the House and his crude reply to Griswold, Gallatin remarked to his wife "that there is but little delicacy in the usual conversation of most Connecticut gentlemen; that they have contracted a habit of saying very hard things, and that considering Lyon as a low-life fellow they were under no restraint in regard to him."

Coit upheld the propriety of Griswold's violent attempt to retaliate for Lyon's insult. To Mrs. Coit he wrote that his associate's "wooden sword" remark to Lyon "had been richly merited" by the latter's "previous conversation." After having been restrained "from beating him on the Instant," Griswold "today . . . did it with great propriety—not while the house was in session but in the house a few minutes before. It was to be sure imprudent in him to have provoked the insult he received but Lyon had no cause to find fault. He had been guilty of abuse far more outrageous." This, Coit observed, "merited contempt, & a silent contempt. Had he apprehended the Consequences" Griswold "doubtless would have treated it with such. Griswold's Conduct has through the whole business been highly to his honour." Then, he added with reference to his wife's penchant for dire apprehensions, "I hope you will feel no alarm for me from hearing of this kind of scrapes among members of Congress. I can assure you there is no kind of danger." [14]

However, on January 4, as the temperature in Congress was rising, he had written his will. After the Griswold-Lyon episode, partisanship raged hotter than ever.

Publicly Coit did not impugn Griswold's judgment or behavior. The Federalists hailed the Norwich Congressman as their champion, indignant at how they had been vilified in the streets and had had mud and dung thrown on their carriages by red-cockade-bedecked "sans-culottes." In Connecticut the Federalists ridiculed Lyon. Communications to the *Courant* conferred the knighthood of "the wooden sword" on the three Massachusetts Congressmen who had voted against his expulsion. Lyon, these predicted, would be promoted to "Knight of the Wooden Horse . . . *dignified,* with a rich Panoply of Tar and Feathers." [15] Griswold's political fortune was made by his feud with Lyon, which more than confirmed prospects derived from his kinship to Senator Hillhouse and the Wolcotts. Eventually he became a United States Senator and subsequently governor of Connecticut during the War of 1812.

Coit, on the other hand, suffered from misrepresentations of his attempt to confine the attempted expulsion of Lyon to his initial insult to Griswold and the House. James Springer's attempt in *The Weekly Oracle* to vindicate him seemed to imply that he had opposed expulsion. Mortified, Coit explained to Perkins that he had attempted to exclude reference to Lyon's indecent language from the expulsion motion to prevent "belittling the subject & ourselves." He sent a statement to correct "the false impressions" to be handed to Springer, hoping that it would seal "the damnation" of the Jacobin *Bee*.[16]

His wife reacted to his report of the Griswold-Lyon combat with a vigorous criticism of politics in general. He replied that he was "not surprised" at her "feelings on the subject." He admitted he could at times "hardly believe my own senses, when they shew me the folly, passions & unreasonableness of the action on our political Theatre." He then observed philosophically, with more poise and

"CONGRESSIONAL PUGILISTS"

Matthew Lyon vs. Roger Griswold, February 15, 1798

From a contemporary cartoon

self-assurance than might have been expected in view of the bitter criticisms directed at him:

> I have learnt to feel myself pretty much at ease. I see much extravagance of party on both sides of me. I have been abused for my moderation but I have not been wounded by anything that has been said of me since the praises of those whom I despised.[17] This world and man who is the principal agent in it are such a strange & heterogeneous Composition that few things ought to excite our surprise. That there are evils in it there is no question. Perhaps however they are only partial and except for the purpose of curing them perhaps we ought never to look at them without considering the (perhaps necessary) Connection they bear to the good. Taking the world all together, & more particularly what I have to do with it, I thank God that he has made such a one and that he has put me in it.— perhaps however I should not be able to say so but for my hopes. These buoy me over many tedious & unpleasant scenes in my present situation.[18]

This was a revealing commentary indeed upon Congress.

Coit voted with the Federalists in their defeat of the Republicans' attempt to repeal the stamp tax, remarking during the debate that there was "no better way of raising money than by a tax of this kind." [19] However, he adhered consistently neither to the pro-British High Federalist element which now regarded French attacks upon American commerce as tantamount to a declaration of war,[20] nor to the bipartisan moderates with whom he had been identified during the preceding session. He scorned the Republicans as "Jacobins" as much as did the ultras of his party. As the partisan tempest rose higher during the ensuing months, his independence placed him in a dangerously exposed position.

To counteract the effects of the Griswold-Lyon affair, the Republicans attacked the Federalist diplomats in an acrimonious attempt to push through the Nicholas amendment to reduce the salaries of all American ministers abroad to $4500 a year, except those at London, Paris, and Madrid. In the midst of this, on February 28, Coit read to the House a long extract from Jefferson's letter to Mazzei. This embarrassed the opposition while inflaming the Federalists. Acidly, he alluded to the "sort of political enthusiasm" which "seemed to take to itself exclusive republicanism," a deft parrying of the criticism of Adams' preference for Federalists in the diplomatic service. Surely the Republicans agreed that those entertaining the letter's sentiments should be debarred from public office, he observed ironically, since "nothing but treason and insurrection would be the consequence of such opinions." Besides, the President's appointing power derived from the people and the House could not control it.

Coit's definition of the issues at stake rallied the Federalists. They defeated all amendments to the foreign intercourse bill by the close vote of 52 to 48. A verbatim report in the *Connecticut Courant* of Coit's speech re-established his reputation for political orthodoxy in Connecticut. He had led the Federalists into effective support of the Adams administration on a vital issue.[21] Ten days after his speech he wrote his wife, "Thank God as to my politics I feel much at ease. Misstatement & misrepresentation of facts I may suffer by momentarially. Generally however I think my Conduct will exhibit what misrepresentation can not long cloud or hide."[22]

Among the High Federalists, resentment against the Republicans' opposition to the foreign intercourse bill was intense. Harrison Gray Otis of Boston wrote home that "if the Southern States do not change their Representation, or that Representation change their measures, that part of the country will be lost, and the Eastern States will be compelled to take care of themselves." Thus the pressure of deepening crisis and acerbating partisanship led him to contemplate the possibility of a Northern confederacy such as the Wolcott faction in Connecticut had offered in 1796 as the alternative to Adams' election. In reply to Coit, Gallatin defended Jefferson's letter to Mazzei, stating that many Americans believed a monarcho-aristocratic faction existed. He attacked the entire Federalist system of diplomacy and commercial treaties.[23]

While Congress awaited the deciphering of recent dispatches from the special mission at Paris, Coit supported the introduction of the provisional army (federal militia) bill desired by the Hamiltonians. He warned Perkins privately against Republican attempts to alienate the public from the Administration. He also led in defeating Rhode Island's attempt to secure federal redemption of its inflated Revolutionary currency. With the other Connecticut members, he provided the margin needed to defeat Edward Livingston's bill to assign interstate litigation to the federal court in the state next adjoining the disputants. This blocked the attempt by New York to secure a settlement favorable to it of a case pending between it and Connecticut. Such actions established further Coit's caliber as a loyal Federalist, standing guard against raids on the federal treasury and his state's interests.[24]

CHAPTER EIGHT

The French War and Civil Liberties

THE partisan battles of the first months of the Fifth Congress' regular session were preliminary to the crisis that was precipitated by the humiliating failure of the special mission to France. All but the High Federalists had hoped for a negotiated settlement, although the Republicans understood better France's opposition to Jay's Treaty and how the Directory would react to C. C. Pinckney's inclusion in the special mission. Only Jefferson's following desired to resuscitate the Franco-American alliance, Talleyrand's major objective. This the composition of the mission made it impossible to accomplish. Prospects for a successful negotiation had been diminished further by the moderates' refusal to support the stronger armaments that Hamilton demanded and by the re-emergence of Northern secessionism within the Federalist Party. Of that Talleyrand was probably informed. In February 1798, news circulated among the Republicans of that figure's informal assurance to Jefferson that France would not declare war in retaliation for Jay's Treaty, although no immediate "arrangement" might be made.[1]

Few Federalists in Congress were prepared, however, for Adams' sensational message of March 19, which announced the mission's failure and recommended immediate preparation for war. He did not transmit the dispatches from his envoys, since such an action might endanger their persons while they remained in France. However, he declared that they could not succeed in the proposed negotiation "on terms compatible with the safety, honor, or the essential interests of the Nation." Simultaneously, Secretary of State Timothy Pickering conveyed to the High Federalists in both houses

Hamilton's insistence upon a formidable armament. This, the former Secretary insisted, should include completion of the frigates, ten ships of the line if actual war developed, privateering, arming of merchant ships, port fortifications, increase of the army to twenty thousand plus a larger provisional army, new taxes to finance this, and Congressional suspension of the treaties of 1778 with France. Adams' more moderate program stressed the navy. The competing armaments proposals provided the chief staple of Congressional proceedings during the next four months.[2]

Privateering or private war by American citizens under government letters of marque and reprisal against the French marine could be an indirect means of precipitating formal war with the victorious French Directory.

Stunned by the President's message, the Republicans in Congress played for time. Incredulous, they demanded transmission of the envoys' dispatches to the House, an attempt to expose the alleged lack of grounds for his alarm. This they claimed derived from domestic politics rather than Paris. John Allen countered with a motion requesting the dispatches. This was passed by the opposing extremes over the opposition of the moderates. Among the latter were Coit, Dana, Goodrich, and Griswold, a majority of the Connecticut delegation, and Otis and Sewall of Massachusetts, who also upheld the wisdom of the President's decision not to transmit them.[3]

After Pickering deleted the names of Talleyrand's intermediaries, whom he identified as Monsieurs X, Y, and Z, Congress received the dispatches on April 3. These included Marshall's famous memorial to Talleyrand, and disclosed that the latter had demanded via the now anonymous agents a large bribe for himself and the Directors and a disguised loan for France such as the Batavian Republic had found it advisable to make recently. The loan would have reduced the United States to satellite status and disrupted Anglo-American relations, which was what the Directory desired. Publication of the documents precipitated an immediate sensation in the United States, and hot indignation at the venal and arrogant attempt to subordinate this nation to the French Republic, whose armies were victorious in Europe. Especially resented were Monsieur Y's threats that the Directory would employ the "French Party" in the United States to overthrow Adams' administration and gain control.

Public opinion rallied promptly behind President Adams. Citizens' meetings sent him a flood of patriotic resolutions, to which he responded with high-spirited, even vitriolic statements. The black cockade of the War of Independence reappeared. Young men joined privately organized volunteer regiments. As the spirit of nationality burgeoned under the stimulus of an apprehended French invasion, America sang Joseph Hopkinson's "Hail Columbia." Patriotism developed unprecedented intensity while Congress labored, and rose to a peak when Marshall landed in New York and received a hero's reception in Philadelphia on June 20–26. After his report to the President, he was honored at a great public dinner whose "crowning toast" was "Millions for defense but not one cent for tribute!" [4] This became the slogan of aroused American nationality.

Meanwhile, Republican strength in Congress melted away, leaving the Federalists in control but divided among themselves. The High or ultra element insisted upon Hamilton's program, protection of the nation from subversion, and formal war with France. The moderate Federalists were less precipitate, more cautious lest they jeopardize the national welfare by excessive armaments or an emotional resort to hostilities that could not be conducted with reasonable hope of success.

The initial policy setting for Congress' work was provided on March 26, before the dispatches were transmitted, by the adoption of the Sprigg Resolutions despite Sewall's objection that a state of war with France already existed. These resolutions declared that while it was *"not expedient* for the United States to resort to war against the French Republic" yet "adequate provision shall be made . . . for the protection of our seacoast, and for the internal defence of the country." [5]

In the House, the Committee for the Defense of the Country and the Protection of Commerce was appointed to draft necessary bills. To it also relevant Senate bills were referred. The chairman was Samuel Sewall. Thus the House anticipated Wolcott's observation to Hamilton on April 5, "A few days will determine whether the Legislature can act with that decision & energy which the Crisis demands." Wolcott envisaged immediate war. Coit hoped that public opinion would now permit arming American merchantmen.

Thereafter, as the House leaders took up the bills reported by the Committee, the Federalist ultras there and outside of Congress followed the example of William Pitt's party in Great Britain, "constantly keeping up an alarm over impending danger in order to stifle all opposition." This tactic obscured the distinction between the "actual danger" of a French invasion of England and the remote possibility of a similar attack upon the United States. As early as May 10, Speaker Dayton informed the House that a French army was being prepared to invade America, not England. This Fenno's *Gazette* corroborated with "authentic information." [6]

Soon the ultras declared that all opposition to their defense program was cowardly and indicative of an intent to fraternize with the enemy, while they tracked down and publicized fictitious "conspiracies" or attacked Republicans in the streets. The opposition in Congress attempted to limit armaments and to avoid giving more offense to France, and declared that the Directory's rejection of the special mission was no *causus belli*. But this the ultras condemned as disloyal. John Allen declared in the House that some Republican members' hatred of "our government leads them to prefer another profligate and ferocious as it is." [7]

Especially resented by Wolcott and his Essex Junto friends were Talleyrand's attempts to assure the Republicans that France did not desire war but wished renewed negotiations and a settlement of differences. This was learned from overseas dispatches to leading Republicans seized from the mails in Boston. Federalist commercial and maritime interests wanted the protection of British convoys and unimpeded access to British markets and finance. Domestically, the High Federalists sought to demoralize and discredit the Republican Party as being the Directory's instrument. Formal war would facilitate this.

The aggressive Federalist war faction included bellicose Boston merchants, the Essex Junto, John Allen of Connecticut, and the Hamiltonians, who dreamed with their leader of retaliation upon France by conquering Florida, Louisiana, and Mexico from Spain, the Directory's ally. The more provincial of this element vented their spleen against the South, terming it dangerously Gallophile. Such was the situation that developed between April 3 and the adjournment of Congress on July 15.[8]

The Federalist moderates were drawn from their bipartisan coalition with the Republican moderates by the ultras' stress upon patriotism and national defense. Speaker Dayton became a vociferous extremist. However, within the reunited Federalists the ex-moderates exerted a restraining influence. At times this was decisive. The struggle over policy continued to be triangular, while the Republicans were weakened by the withdrawal of some members to their constituencies.[9]

The President's limited defense program communicated by Sewall to the House gratified the Federalist moderates. For this the Hamiltonians attempted strenuously to substitute their own.[10] Coit was obliged repeatedly to choose which to support on specific measures as they came before the House, and was enabled thereby to continue his course as an independent Federalist of moderate views.

His activity during the X Y Z crisis can now be described. Like Dayton, he became a vigorous proponent of strong measures, although not as extreme nor virulent as was John Allen. Native caution, the habit of independent thinking, and a different conception of national interest led Coit at times to oppose the ultras' policies decisively.

He did not speak on the bill to add twenty-two ships to the navy. Although he voted against his state delegation and most Federalists to reduce the number of sloops of war from sixteen to twelve, he voted with them in the Committee of the Whole to defeat Gallatin's amendment to prevent their use in convoying. He voted for the revised bill. He extended this reversal of his position of the year before when he helped his party to create the Department of the Navy by a margin of 47 to 41. He voted vainly with the Hamiltonians for a three-year provisional army of twenty thousand. When it was reduced to ten thousand and limited in duration until "the next Congress," he supported this, an action which the influential *Middlesex Gazette* of Middletown, Connecticut, impliedly approved.[11]

Coit voted on June 1 with the Federalist majority to suspend commercial intercourse with France. In retaliation for Gallatin's opposition to this action, he secured postponement of the extension of the federal district courts to Kentucky and Tennessee, a thrust at the pro-French West. He concurred in the consolidation of all military appropriations into a single bill. He supported the valuation of lands and houses, and the enumeration of slaves, for direct taxation. He defended the direct tax to raise $2,000,000 in new revenue to finance new armaments.[12]

Then he sided with Adams in opposing the increase of the army from eight to twelve regiments, producing a tie vote that Dayton resolved in favor of the increase. Coit voted for the amended army bill. On May 31, the day after the navy and provisional army bills became law, he defeated Gallatin's attempt to postpone the bill to increase the compensation of internal revenue collectors, which

Secretary Wolcott desired. Coit attempted vainly to exempt merchants from having to give bond that their ships would observe the non-intercourse act.[13]

A month earlier, in late April, he had gone home for a brief visit with his heavily burdened wife. A week in New London sufficed to restore her morale and renew his excellent rapport with their children. He consulted with Perkins, Captain Bulkeley, the Hallams, other Union Bank friends, merchants, and visiting farmers. No doubt he received an appraisal of political currents from Samuel Green of the *Gazette*. At the last moment, he secured some porter for his family and jumped on the stage for New York and Philadelphia.[14]

While in New London, he must have probed the attitude of eastern Connecticut on the issue of peace or war with France. A month earlier, on March 23, he had written to the Reverend Stanley Griswold of New Milford that he opposed a war to gratify prejudice. This correspondence appeared in the *Connecticut Courant* on May 21 and disclosed also Coit's lack of sympathy with the Republican position. By identifying himself publicly as a moderate and informing the war Federalists of his opposition to their cherished objective, he incurred their implacable enmity. This publication ensured his defeat for re-election, Coit believed.

Their opposition was strengthened by his defeat of the Foster Resolution to authorize privateering. He opposed the initial motion to refer this to Sewall's committee, admitting that he was "embarrassed on this subject." He did not anticipate a favorable negotiation with France "that will ensure peace." He "believed we should have war; but he did not wish to go on faster to this state of things than the people of this country, and the opinion of the world would justify." He deduced realistically that the resolution was an indirect method of precipitating war with France. While drawing attention to this, he implied that there was an advantage to awaiting France's expected attack, and envisaged apparently the advantage of waging a defensive war with unified public support. When beaten on his motion to delay consideration, he cast the deciding vote against the resolution, having combined the moderates including Dana with Gallatin's following. This inflicted a severe defeat upon the war Federalists.[15]

Subsequently, on the last day of the session, he again defeated privateering, which Cabot favored, by casting the deciding vote against authorization of a bounty on the guns of French armed vessels captured by privately armed American ships. Some of these were commissioned by the President under another act of Congress.

Consequently, although Congress directed the navy's three frigates and the new sloops of war to engage in hostilities with French warships and privateers off the American coast and in the West Indies, a widespread attack by inumerable American privateers upon French shipping did not materialize.[16] The absence of such extensive American privateering during the brief Naval War with France made it easier for Talleyrand to notify President Adams via the American Minister at The Hague that he would receive an American Minister empowered to negotiate a general settlement. To this extent, Coit's partial defeat of privateering facilitated the settlement of 1799–1800 on honorable and advantageous terms.

He made this contribution to an eventual peaceful settlement of the crisis at the cost of alienating the maritime interests of Connecticut and elsewhere from himself. Many shipowners were anticipating lucrative profits from privateering. Although he was no doubt influenced by his indifference to further Congressional service, Coit must have known that his action diminished the opportunity to enter trade or banking as an alternative to the bar, and that it might jeopardize the Brainerd and Coit law practice.

William Cobbett, journalistic spokesman of the war Federalists, attacked him bitterly after he defeated the Foster Resolution as "the balancing Mr. Coit." To him Cobbett preferred "a 'known Democrat' . . . I would sooner vote for Callender [17] than Coit" because his "superabundant vanity" was "of no earthly use but to drag out a session of Congress, tantalize the people, and put the Executive to an unnecessary expense." Connecticut voters, the *Porcupine* declared, should exclude him from Congress.[18]

However, Coit did not reject the possibility of having to fight France. This his speech on the Foster Resolution indicated. On June 16 he wrote to his son Bob also:

> If we have to fight the Frenchmen we shall have a great deal of work to do, and as they go on at present it seems they are determined we shall give them all the property they please to ask for & let them do with us as they have a mind. this will not do. *'Tis certainly more honourable & better to fight them.*[19]

Three weeks later, after the Naval War began, he sent Bob some Philadelphia newspapers. He added:

> By those I enclose you will see that we have got one French Privateer —if we have a war with the Frenchmen & it should last a few years you will grow big enough I hope to help fight them. What think you should you make a good Soldier? [20]

Coit obviously expected a long defensive war resulting from overt French aggression.

This explains also why he helped to defeat a precipitate Congressional declaration of war. Even Fisher Ames, who demanded heavier armaments and thorough measures, restricted his recommendation to Pickering to "a full state of *war,* waged but not *declared,* and limited cautiously to the existence of their vile acts" as the appropriate action to be taken by Congress. Almost simultaneously, Hamilton recommended that the United States "act with spirit and energy as well towards G Britain as France":

> I would *mete* the same measure to both of them. . . . One of them will quickly court us—and by this course of conduct our Citizens will be enthusiastically united to the Government. It will evince that

we are neither *Greeks* nor *Trojans*. In very critical cases bold expedients are often necessary.

Hamilton believed that Pitt's government would seek an alliance that would facilitate vigorous measures against France and its allies. Pickering was soon convinced that "War is inevitable" because of the collapse of the Paris negotiation, and he informed a relative that "we shall most assuredly go into all the preparations for a certain war." However, Stephen Higginson had reported to Pickering that in Massachusetts "some new Event" was needed to arouse popular patriotism to a point that would lead it to support "exertions which our situation requires." New Englanders were "not so much roused at present as in the Southern States," he added. Coit's caution, therefore, was based upon a realistic appreciation of the state of public opinion in his region.

After prearrangement with the Massachusetts Federalists and concurrent with a prediction of a declaration of war in the *Columbian Centinel,* John Allen introduced a resolution to declare war on France in the House on July 4. Sewall joined Coit in rallying sufficient support to defeat this without a roll call, for the obvious reason that a *causus belli* was lacking. So bitter was the resentment exhibited against him after this by the war faction that Coit wrote "July 4, 1798" upon his undated will of the preceding January. From the beginning of the war scare, he had envisaged the conflict as resulting from French aggression. He did not believe it wise for the United States to declare war before it was attacked, although he thought a clash was inevitable.

Then a secret caucus was called of the Federalists in Congress. At that meeting Coit, Sewall, and their friends defeated the war faction's demand for absolute cooperation and a declaration of war. However, on July 6 Coit had voted with his party to void the two treaties of 1778 with France, thereby terminating the Franco-American alliance and the commercial advantages that it had brought to the United States.

His leadership of the moderate Federalists was decisive in preventing a precipitate declaration of war before Congress adjourned. This explains why he was singled out for attack by the bellicose Stephen Higginson of Salem on July 11 in a letter to Secretary Wolcott:

> It is impossible for the government to get along whilst its friends are so divided and the opposition so firm and united. In times like the present, when dangers, novel in their kind and terrible in their aspect, press us on every side, it is provoking to hear men talk of their independence, their candour, their love of conciliation, and their aversion to party like Mr. Coit.[21]

Coit must have expressed this viewpoint at social gatherings in Philadelphia.

Higginson had advised Wolcott earlier that war was "the only safe situation possible to be taken in the present state of things," and that a declaration could be obtained by vigorous executive leadership.[22] John Allen was bitter at the moderates' defeat of his objective. He remarked heatedly, as if expressing continued faith of the Wolcott faction in contingent secession, "I sometimes think it impossible for this government to last long and if we must be forever tormented with these rascals, the present government is not worth anything," while alluding bluntly to "the opposition to the government by Jacobins within doors and without." [23]

In view of this, it can be seen that Coit's partial defeat of privateering and of a formal declaration of war indicated also his continuing opposition to contingent Northern secession, all of which the Wolcotts' Litchfield Junto favored. Since *The Bee* likewise opposed those three policies, it was evident that Coit and Holt represented New London's opposition to disunion and the precipitate war of Allen and his sponsors. To Allen, Coit was obviously a "Jacobin within doors" and Holt a "Jacobin . . . without." The former's phrase was evidently an attempt to obscure the fact that in opposing both of the war faction's legislative proposals Coit had received the support of the Adams Federalists or moderates. His determination that the United States must await attack was cautious, considerably short of the rising patriotic spirit. Marshall had learned, however, that Talleyrand and Pitt were negotiating. If England made peace after America declared war on France, the superior power of the latter's fleet would have laid the United States open to invasion by the irresistible French armies, of which Napoleon was the rising star. Talleyrand was already negotiating with Madrid for the return of Louisiana to France, rumors of which must have reached the State Department.[24]

Coit's calm, independent opposition to precipitate war, and his success in combining the moderate Federalists with the Republicans to defeat it, contrasted vividly with Hamilton's subsequently disclosed desire to employ the reluctant army to conquer the Spanish colonies in North America. So far as he could do so, Coit applied to the X Y Z crisis of 1798 the policy of non-involvement in European wars that he had upheld so conspicuously during 1794 and 1796. While defeating precipitate, immediate war with its great risk, Coit implicitly revealed also that he would fight the war Federalists' policy of contingent secessionism if need be.

He knew, although most Americans have long since forgotten it, that "Pelham" had returned to the *Courant's* columns that spring while "Gustavus" continued to second his advocacy of Northern secession and organization of a regional federal union. The *Courant* was the chief journalistic organ of the Yale-Litchfield leadership. Already those essayists were supplying some of the "antidotes" for the propaganda of "Jacobin demagogues," as they dubbed the Republican leaders who were attempting to capture the entire state Congressional delegation.[25] He may have realized that formal war with France would have made the United States the *de facto* ally of Great Britain,[26] for which he entertained no great affection. Furthermore, he exhibited no desire for the territorial aggrandizement of the United States. At the same time he was strongly opposed to the Republicans, whom he also called "Jacobins." In this position can be discerned the viewpoint of the New London Federalists whose city had been burned by Britain in 1781 and which was still open to attack from the sea.

When the chips were down during the X Y Z crisis, therefore, Coit was neither an Anglophile Hamiltonian chauvinist nor a Gallophile Jeffersonian. Instead, he won as a cautious, realistic, American Federalist, who weighed carefully the cost of taking a divided nation precipitately into war with the world's greatest military power and second-greatest naval power. Judging from the favorable popular reaction in 1799 to Adams' decision to renew negotiations with France and avoid formal war, in defiance of the Hamiltonians, Coit's position was politically comprehensible. That he contributed measurably to the national welfare in 1798 by defeating both privateering initially and a declaration of war became apparent when the risks of both were weighed.

What, however, was Coit's attitude toward the war Federalists' attempt to introduce into the United States the Pitt government's suppression of internal dissent and political opposition so as to prevent subversion and radical insurrection?

Both the Adams and the Hamiltonian Federalists were apprehensive lest the Directory's intrigues and the political activity of radical *émigrés* in the United States unite with the influence of French radicalism and the turbulent Irish immigrants in a revolutionary movement. From this viewpoint it was patriotic and wise to suppress or oust such dangerous elements. Their activity had already fostered the development of a well-defined nativism among the Federalists of both factions. To restrain the "democratic" elements, Federalist judges were enforcing English common law penalties for libel and conspiracy as part of an alleged federal common law. Federalist leaders cognizant of the open liaison of successive French Ministers to the United States with the Republican leaders, and of the journalistic and political activity of French and Irish immigrants and such English radicals as Joseph Priestley in the Republican Party, confused political opposition with subversion, a not entirely unrealistic attitude.

Before publication of the X Y Z papers, but privy to their contents, Senator Sedgwick declared privately that they presented "a glorious opportunity to destroy faction. Improve it." The High Federalists attempted to do this and to win universal support for their policy by advocating restriction of naturalization, control of aliens, and the elimination of political criticism in imitation of William Pitt's system. While studying his recently renewed Alien Law, Seditious Meetings Law, and Treasonable Practices Law, they continued to imitate his tactic of keeping up a continual alarm against alleged radical plots.[27] This policy developed concomitantly with the attempt to secure Congressional adoption of the Hamiltonian armament program and of the precipitate war policy.

Coit initiated the Federalists' domestic legislative program. That developed swiftly into an adaptation of Pitt's system. On April 17, after passage of the bill for an additional regiment of artillery and engineers, Coit rose in the House and remarked that "from the present situation of things, he apprehended some alterations would be necessary in the present law for the naturalization of foreigners." He proposed that the Committee for the Defense of the Country and the Protection of Commerce "be directed to enquire and report whether it be not expedient to suspend or to amend the act establishing a universal rule of naturalization." The nativist and antisubversion implications of this were immediately grasped. Jefferson reported to Madison that this was the beginning of the enactment of the program of the "war party" in a special attempt to "reach" Gallatin, his lieutenant.[28]

Samuel Sitgreaves of Pennsylvania insisted successfully during the discussion of Coit's resolution that because of the "immense number of French citizens in our country" at "a time when we may be shortly involved in war," consideration of regulations for resident aliens be included. The amended resolution with its dual objective passed *unanimously,* evidence that upon this all factions and parties in the House were agreed. Although the Federalist ultras did not remark upon it, the Republicans present reacted to these issues as Americans, not Francophiles. They and the Federalist moderates agreed that the national emergency demanded precautions against subversion by aliens and naturalized citizens. During the debate, the attempts of Frenchmen in Kentucky and elsewhere to alienate citizens from the government were cited as justification for Sitgreaves' amendment.[29]

All knew of the fate of Holland and Switzerland and their current humiliating role as French satellites. The bitter public resentment at Talleyrand's intimation, via Monsieur Y, that America would welcome reduction to this status made it necessary for the Republicans to disinfect themselves by disassociation with the French *émigrés* and immigrant Irish revolutionaries. The cynical, venal French Foreign Minister, who had resided a few years earlier in the United States as an *émigré,* underestimated the force of American nationalism. This miscalculation affected decisively but adversely to the French Republic the orientation of the party that he regarded as the tool of his designs.

Although recent authorities relate the Federalists' naturalization and alien policies to American civil liberties, it should be observed that no foreign resident in any nation possessed at that time the privilege of entering into politics, whether innocently or with the intent to subvert the government. While the well-publicized activities of French, Irish, and English immigrants in the Democratic Clubs and Republican Party made the issue clear, it should be noted that William Cobbett, editor of *Porcupine's Gazette* and the *Country Porcupine* in Philadelphia in behalf of the Federalists, was an unnaturalized English immigrant. The silence of the national Bill of

Rights on the rights of aliens other than the safeguards that it granted to "the people," and Congress' complete authority over naturalization requirements, indicated to the Federalists a clear field within which it could act. Coit's leadership in initiating naturalization legislation was that of an American Federalist.

On May 1, Sewall reported three resolutions from his committee. They proposed legislation requiring longer residence for naturalization, a system of registration and reporting for aliens, and authorization to the President to deport enemy aliens. This was the House's contribution to the Federalist domestic program. It produced, after debate and Senate assistance, three laws. These were a new Naturalization Act, an Alien Act, and an Enemy Alien Act. An interim demand by Federalist ultras that citizenship and federal offices be limited to the native born was adjudged unconstitutional.

During the debate on the naturalization bill reported on May 21, Coit defeated Gallatin's attempt to exempt from it aliens who had arrived before January 26, 1795. He cast the deciding vote for a fourteen-year residence requirement for naturalization, nearly three times as long as the existing one.[30] Then, instead of backing Sewall's milder version, he supported Senator Hillhouse's more stringent enemy alien bill emphatically, which John Allen substituted with bipartisan support for the House bill after the Republican *Aurora* of Philadelphia published Talleyrand's conciliatory letter to the envoys of the special mission without official permission. Coit voted also for the House alien bill, which provided for registration of aliens during peace. Its majority support came almost entirely from the Northern Congressmen. Coit was uninfluenced by Livingston's powerful attack upon the Alien Bill and Alien Enemy Bill, which rallied the Republicans.[31]

Moneieur Y's arrogant threat to Marshall, Pinckney, and Gerry that the Directory would place the *"French party"* in control of the United States, which John Allen quoted before the House, led to the introduction of sedition bills there and in the Senate. These presented the issue of possible civil rights infringements in an inescapable form to the discredited Republicans. The danger in the situation, which Senator James Lloyd's bill made evident, was that the Federalists' desire to suppress genuine subversion and "faction" alike might lead them into such a repression of the opposition as would precipitate a decisive reaction in its favor. Lloyd's bill reproduced the British law of political libel so completely that if enacted and enforced it would have extinguished the Republican Party. His objective undoubtedly was to duplicate Pitt's success in reducing the political opposition to "a coach load of Whigs." [32]

Hamilton protested effectively against so Draconian a policy. His friends in the House, Otis, Harper, and James A. Bayard, succeeded in modifying Lloyd's bill drastically. The resulting law might have been even less stringent had not Benjamin Franklin Bache published in the *Aurora* Talleyrand's conciliatory letter, which discredited the Federalist claim that France was plotting war against the United States. This journalistic coup was cited hotly in Congress as justification for duplicating Britain's stringent press curbs.

Coit was caught up in this wave of indignation and partisan intolerance. When the House managers proposed jury trials under the modified bill, he and Griswold voted vainly against this amendment. Yeas and nays were not taken on the vitally important amendment to admit the truth of a publication as a defense in court. Coit's vote for the amended bill enabled the Federalists to pass it in the House by the narrow margin of 44 to 41. This was too small to give the measure, which President Adams signed on July 14, the moral force needed to ensure general popular approval. [33] It was this measure that infringed upon the spirit if not the letter of the First Amendment to the Constitution.

Until then, the disclosure by the X Y Z dispatches of conclusive evidence of a dangerous liaison between the French Directory and the Republican Party had discredited the latter in the opinion of the aroused public. However, the national Bill of Rights had been necessary to secure popular approval of the federal Constitution and acceptance by the Antifederalists. The Sedition Law's impairment of freedom of speech and the press, ostensibly in an attempt to restrain the criticism of public officials, and the move on the part of the Federalist ultras to destroy the Republican Party gave the latter a priceless issue. When combined with the bitter struggle between the Adams and Hamiltonian factions within the Federalist Party, the subsequent disclosure of Hamilton's unpopular imperialist policy, and Adams' renewal of negotiations with Talleyrand in 1799, the enforcement of the Sedition Act enabled Jefferson and his lieutenants to rehabilitate their party. Thus that Act helped to pave the way for the "Revolution of 1800" that deprived the Federalists permanently of national power.[34] Undoubtedly Coit's antipathy to Charles Holt's *Bee* in New London led him to support Lloyd's sedition bill and to resist its weakening while it was before the House. In this manner he contributed to one of the most notable Pyrrhic legislative victories in American history.

Holt denounced the sedition bill when it was before the House in *The Bee*. If enacted, he predicted, it would reduce the Constitution to "a mere *dead letter*" by contravening "the code of freedom" in the Bill of Rights. It would be employed to enforce "presidential infallibility." Thus he embarked upon the course of opposition and vigorous criticism of the Adams administration that led to his indictment and conviction under the Sedition Law in 1800. Of special interest in his editorial articles on that measure during 1798 was the disclosure that, during the debate in the House, Congressmen introduced protesting letters from their constituents and cited the opposing speeches of fellow members as justification for its enactment. This, Holt asserted accurately, was proof that the new law's intent was to deny indispensable civil rights to opponents of the Administration.[35]

Thus, before Coit traveled by stage from Philadelphia to New

London in mid-July, his local journalistic opponent had capitalized upon the issues of civil liberties and the right of the political opposition to criticize the party in power which this last of the Federalists' four domestic acts presented to the Jeffersonians. His support of these measures indicated how far Coit had been swept from the moderate liberalism of his and his party's earlier years by the sudden burgeoning of the war spirit, the patriotism apprehensive of subversion by the French version of the present-day "Fifth Column," and the extreme Federalist partisanship that would destroy all "faction" but its own.

CHAPTER NINE

An Untimely Exit

IRONICALLY, Coit's support of the High Federalists' domestic program left them unreconciled to him. They resented bitterly his and Sewall's defeat of the immediate declaration of war. They resented Coit's partial defeat of privateering, the indirect method of achieving formal war with France that would be so profitable presumably to shipowners. They resented his defiance in the House of their attempt to prescribe a rigid party orthodoxy and loyalty, not so much by his words as by his votes and, no doubt, his quiet influence in committees and outside the bar of the House. His leadership of the moderate Federalists and his influence with the moderate Republicans represented a third force in American politics and in Congress, which the Federalist ultras were determined to eliminate. In other words, it was not so much his speeches as his power that they resented, in addition to his defeat of precipitate war and the alliance with Britain which they desired.

In Connecticut, there were other reasons for the ultras' dislike of him. There was his refusal to follow the leadership of Secretary Wolcott, for a few months acting head of the Navy Department as well as permanent, hard-working chief of the Treasury. Coit's attempts to reduce the naval and military authorizations were a direct challenge to the Hamiltonians. To the Wolcott leadership, his implied opposition to its contingent secessionism was also intolerable.

Coit's moderate position on the armament program and his opposition to privateering were actions that could be turned against him in a state whose industries, shipbuilders, and shipowners expected to profit from the defense programs of either the Administration or Hamilton. Since he had supported the four domestic acts of the Federalists' program and thereby demonstrated his political orthodoxy, only his anti-privateering stand and his attempt to reduce the number of sloops of war could be invoked to discredit him with the freemen. Furthermore, it could be insinuated that Coit was liked and his Congressional moderation appreciated by Gideon Granger and other Republican leaders who were now organizing openly in Connecticut. Their clinging to his coattails in a pre-primary campaign, while attempting to draw away the support formerly given him by Francophile freemen, was politically embarrassing to him, as he well knew.

The attempt to eliminate Coit from the Congressional delegation began with the X Y Z crisis in the spring. Although he had already been nominated near the head of the list for re-election, the party leaders rejected that action of the freemen. In April they asked them to nominate a new slate, after the Republicans had ascertained by means of Coit's exchange of letters with the Reverend Mr. Griswold of New Milford that he was opposed to a war with France based "upon prejudice." On Election Day the new list of Congressional nominees was headed by Goodrich, Wolcott's brother-in-law. Coit ranked ninth on the list, below two new men, while the other Congressmen ranked sufficiently high to ensure their re-election.[1]

Thus Coit appeared to be scheduled for retirement *before* his course in Congress during June–July aroused more intense hostility among members of the Federalist war faction. He understood the implications of his drastically reduced rank on the nomination list, and the political consequences of his determination to prevent a precipitate war.

On June 11, the day he defeated the Foster Resolution on privateering, he wrote to Mrs. Coit to prepare her for the termination of his Congressional career, the event for which she hoped. This prospect he attributed exclusively to the situation in Connecticut and especially to the withdrawal from him of "three or four hundred

Jacobin votes," whose support the other Congressmen had not enjoyed, for the benefit of the opposition. This, he informed her, placed him "still lower on the list." He wished "no such support" as those lost votes. Furthermore, "The Jacobins hold me up as one of them & perhaps led others to think falsely of my politics." Assuming that the Republicans would continue to oppose him, he concluded that he would not be re-elected in October when the legislature met in New Haven. "According to my present impressions I should immediately resign & then you would find me restored to home & you."

This he did not do, but remained in Congress to defeat the war faction. What his wishes were on the subject of re-election he was "really at a loss" to describe. He added candidly and revealingly in his letter to his wife:

> I want to get out from where I am so much that I am not certain that the event I contemplate would be desirable. To have lost the Confidence of my Employers with a consciousness of fault would have been mortifying—extremely so—to have lost it anyhow would be mortifying, but that I desire a consolation from a persuasion that meriting it, I shall regain it, & perhaps with some evidences more satisfactory than my present employment affords. You will not mention these things at present. I have not spoken of them to anyone & am not determined whether I ought to.[2]

Probably he expected to be given a federal appointment or a place on the bench of the Superior Court such as was occupied by his friend Zephaniah Swift, the first moderate Federalist of the Connecticut Congressional delegation. How well founded his slightly incoherent hope was that his political fortunes would revive cannot be ascertained. If this was his objective, his immediate task was to regain the confidence and support of a larger proportion of the freemen. For him this was especially difficult because of his deist religious views. Dwight's leadership in the religious reaction and the changed political situation demanded more conformity and party loyalty than he was disposed to concede in Congress. Since he went on between June 11 and July 14 to employ his leadership of the Adams Federalists to defeat the ultras' war policy, he may have anticipated a subsequent appreciation of the wisdom of this course. His leadership in the modification of the Adams naval program and his refusal to support the full strength of the army that Hamilton demanded, together with his support of the Sedition Law that alienated Republican friends, had left him somewhat isolated among the Federalists.

Whether he acted wisely or not, Coit sacrificed his Congressional career and very possibly his political future because of his cautious, courageous integrity during the X Y Z crisis in the field of armaments and foreign policy. Almost certainly, he also injured his law practice and jeopardized whatever opportunity he may have enjoyed to embark upon a business career. He returned home a lonely figure. For the present, his financial status depended upon returns from his Union Bank stock, holdings in government securities, and law practice.

However, his course in Congress must have commanded considerable approval in Connecticut. This explains the continued attacks made upon him in the *Courant* that summer. That paper's editors did not waste ammunition upon the politically dead. Its anonymous reporter of Congressional proceedings (Goodrich) attacked him on July 23 for alleged vacillation on privateering. "It is to be hoped that the firm, decisive and federal people of Connecticut, will not suffer this man any longer to call himself their representative," that reporter added in imitation of Cobbett.

Coit's continued unwillingness to support the Wolcott policy line explains "A Freeman's" communication to the *Courant* of September 3. That contributor demanded Coit's exclusion from Congress "at this time" while conceding that he "is a very honest good man" and "federal in his politics." However, he "is not uniformly so. . . . But now it is absolutely necessary to have such men in Congress who will *always* vote right . . . and not be influenced through whim or caprice—or even through mistake, to vote contrary to our feelings and interest." During the previous session, "A Freeman" added significantly, Coit had voted *"several times* in such a manner as to weaken *defensive measures of government."*

Coit had remained publicly silent, willing to let matters take their course, preoccupied with domestic problems arising from the birth of his sixth child. He retained his law partnership with Brainerd and apparently resumed his practice. He resided in his home on the outskirts of New London.

Then, without local precedent, the terrible yellow fever epidemic that had broken out again in Philadelphia swept north along the coast. It invaded New York, New London, Providence, Boston, and Portsmouth, when those busy ports were bending every effort to complete and man the enlarged navy and fill the new regiments. Viewing the pestilence in retrospect a few months later, Charles Holt of *The Bee* declared that a mass exodus from the afflicted cities, a temporary suspension of port and shipbuilding activity, and a general fear of the mysteriously fatal malady had deflated the war spirit.[3]

Among the fever's earliest victims in New London was the popular Captain Elijah Bingham, a Mason and keeper of the Union Coffee House. On that Sunday, August 26, the Union Lodge assembled at his funeral as the local population fled in such panic that it left its livestock behind uncared for. A four-man Health Committee and the courageous Doctor Samuel H. P. Lee remained with the afflicted along the Embankment and up Golden and State Streets to Union Street, the area to which the epidemic was confined.

Either on the occasion of Bingham's funeral, or a few days later when he went into the city to attend to necessary business, Coit contracted the fever. He soon became fatally ill. He was buried before September 5, when the *Connecticut Gazette* included him in its first list of fatalities. He was nearly forty-one years of age when he died.

It remained for Holt, his Republican journalistic antagonist, to publish the best contemporary estimate of him. This he did in the complete list of New London fatalities after the conclusion of the epidemic in his interesting *Short Account of Yellow-Fever as It Appeared in New-London.* Holt observed, after Coit's name, that he was "a gentleman of smooth and polished manner, firm and dignified behaviour, pure and unshaken principles—an able statesman, upright patriot, and respected citizen." [4]

A short while later there was placed above his grave in Cedar Grove Cemetery a granite shaft bearing an inscription that paid tribute to the cultivated, philanthropic liberalism that had distinguished his life:

> If a mind highly cultivated and richly endowed,
> A soul replete with every virtue.
> A heart of universal philanthropy,
> And manners of peculiar affability,
> Will justify an eulogium,
> None who intimately knew him
> Will censure this. [5]

Coit's passing marked in Connecticut the close of a short era in which cosmopolitan, eighteenth-century liberalism dominated intellectual and religious life and when a semi-independent Federalist gentleman, so oriented and essentially American, could achieve political prominence. Thereafter, his former friends Uriah Tracy and Roger Griswold hewed closely to the Wolcott polity, so much so that in a short time both sought to implement the contingent secessionism that the Wolcott faction had enunciated and propagated during 1796–1798. [6] Coit's deft but indirect opposition to this had been not the least among his important activities of those years.

Coit left behind him a young wife and six children, the oldest of whom was twelve. He left his property to his widow "for the benefit of my family." His will, probated on November 19, 1798, bequeathed property described in a subsequent appraisal. This listed a well-equipped house, fifty-six shares of Union Bank stock, a share of Bank of the United States stock, unidentified "Stock in public funds," five shares of Niantic "Feary Bridge" stock, a share in the New London Library, and seventy-five ounces of silver plate.[7]

Notes

Publication details concerning the
works mentioned in these notes, or
the location of manuscript sources,
will be found in the Bibliography.

CHAPTER ONE

A Young Gentleman of New London: Harvard 1776

1. *Diary of Joshua Hempstead of New London, Connecticut, September, 1711, to November, 1758,* 710.

2. Glenn Weaver, *Jonathan Trumbull, Connecticut's Merchant Magistrate,* 49–50; Frances Manwaring Caukins, *History of New London,* 665.

3. *Ibid.,* 476, 502–503; Shaw-Perkins Papers, deed, N. Shaw Jr. to Edward Tinker, August 8, 1769; Arthur Meier Schlesinger, *The Colonial Merchants and the American Revolution, 1763–1776,* 240–252; Weaver, *op. cit.,* 66; F. W. Chapman, *The Coit Family,* 30–31; Mary E. Perkins, *Old Houses of Norwich, 1660–1800,* 58; Miscellaneous Manuscripts, Yale University Library, G. Saltonstall, Jeremiah Miller, and Joseph Coit to Reverend Naptalia Daggett, April 7, 1755; Charles Dyer Parkhurst, compiler, *New London, Connecticut and Vicinity, Early Families,* VI, 146, 155, 157, 165, 175.

4. Caukins, *op. cit.,* 476; William B. Weeden, *Economic and Social History of New England,* II, 757–758.

5. Cf. Weeden, *op. cit.,* II, 731–733.

6. S. Leroy Blake, *Later History of the First Church of New London, Conn.,* 137–163; Caukins, *op. cit.,* 478, 490, 497–498.

7. Weaver, *op. cit.,* 27.

8. Blake, *op. cit.,* 173–174; Caukins, *op. cit.,* 499–503.

9. Joshua Coit Papers, October 14, 1771.

10. Blake, *op. cit.,* 295; Caukins, *op. cit.,* 669.

11. Weaver, *op. cit.,* 25, 29, 141.

12. Harvard University Archives, MS "The Laws of Harvard College, [1767]," 1; MS "Records of the College Faculty," II, 206–207.

13. *Ibid.,* MS "Laws of Harvard College," Ch. II.

14. Quoted in Weeden, *op. cit.,* II, 742.

15. Harvard University Archives, MS "Laws of Harvard College," Chs. II–III.

16. *Ibid.,* "Laws," *passim;* MS "College Records," II, 328–329.

17. *Ibid.,* MS "Records of the College Faculty," IV, 18; *ibid.,* Speaking Club MS "Minutes and Other Records," 1, *passim;* Samuel Eliot Morison, *Three Centuries of Harvard, 1636–1936,* 135–139, 141; Merle Curti, *Growth of American Thought,* 103–132; Franklin Dexter, editor, *The Literary Diary of Ezra Stiles, President of Yale College,* III, 172; James Truslow Adams, *Revolutionary New England, 1691–1776,* 140, 198; Weeden, *op. cit.,* II, 672, 714, 726; Samuel A. Eliot, *A Sketch of the History of Harvard College and of Its Present State,* 80–81.

18. Morison, *op. cit.,* 141.

19. Harvard University Archives, Samuel Chandler MS Diary; Morison, *op. cit.,* 133–135.

20. MSS Letters of Joshua Coit to Daniel Lathrop Coit, Joshua Coit to Mrs. Lucy Huntington, May 10, 1773; Harvard University Archives, MS "Records of the College Faculty," III, 256; William Coolidge Lane, editor, *Letters of Nathaniel Walker Appleton to His Classmate Eliphalet Pearson, 1773–1784,* 293–295; Morison, *op. cit.,* 145–146.

21. Harvard University Archives, MS "College Records," II, 412, 414; Weeden, *op. cit.,* II, 739.

22. Harvard University Archives, MS "Records of the College Faculty," IV, 4–5.

23. *Ibid.,* IV, 12; MS "College Records," II, 433–434.

24. *Ibid.,* MS "Records of the College Faculty," IV, 13–14; Morison, *op. cit.,* 147–149.

25. Harvard University Archives, The Speaking Club MS "Minutes and Other Records," I, *passim;* MS "Catalogue of the Members of the Patriotic Association of Harvard University. From the time of its Foundation, Sept. 1770"; Edmund S. Morgan, *The Birth of the Republic,* 96–97.

26. Harvard University Archives, MS "Records of the College Faculty," IV, 9–10.

27. *Ibid.,* MS "Records," IV, 14–18, 20–22, 25.

28. *Ibid.,* MS "Records," IV, 30; MS "College Records," II, 433–434, 436, 439; Morison, *op. cit.,* 149–151.

29. Harvard University Archives, MS "College Records," II, 442–443; *Catalogus Eorum qui in Collegio Harvardino,* 32.

30. *Ibid.,* title page.

31. MSS Letters of Joshua Coit to Daniel L. Coit, J. Coit to D. L. Coit, February 20, 1779; Papers of Jeremiah Gates Brainerd and Joshua Coit, 1779–1863; Caukins, *op. cit.,* 476, 502, 506, 619; Perkins, *op. cit.,* 160–162; Chapman, *op. cit.,* 58–60.

32. *Ibid.;* Blake, *op. cit.,* 179, 182–208.

33. Weeden, *op. cit.,* II, 779; Weaver, *op. cit.,* 106, 133; Merrill Jensen, *The Articles of Confederation,* 38–39; Caukins, *op. cit.,* 551–556.

34. Oliver Wolcott Papers, Richard Law to Oliver Wolcott Sr., May 9, 1796; Shaw-Perkins Papers, Isaac Wharton to Nathaniel Shaw Jr., February 9, 1782; Ernest E. Rogers, *Connecticut Naval Office at New London during the War of the American Revolution* (New London County Historical Society, *Collections,* II), 11; Charles Allyn, *The Battle of Groton Heights,* 147–149, and *passim;* Leonard Labaree, editor, *Records of the State of Connecticut,* IV, 137, V, 113, 300, 321; Caukins, *op. cit.,* 502, 504, 540–545.

35. Blake, *op. cit.,* 187–190; Shaw-Perkins Papers, Lottery tickets of 1784, Lottery Book, New London Meeting House, June 16, 1787; First Church of Christ, Congregational, New London, MS Archives, First Ecclesiastical Society Records, John Stubbens' receipt to Joshua Coit *et al.,* November 12, 1782, Subscription Paper for Supporting Public Preaching, October 2, 1782, New Meeting House Subscription Paper for Completion of the Meeting House, June 28, 1788.

36. MSS Letters of Joshua Coit to Daniel L. Coit, J. Coit to D. L. Coit, May 31, 1783, April 4, June 1, 1784; Coit Papers, MS appraisal of estate of Joshua Coit; Weaver, *op. cit.,* 28. Cf. *Connecticut Gazette,* January 19, 1792.

CHAPTER TWO
A Novitiate in Connecticut Politics

1. James Truslow Adams, *New England in the Republic, 1776–1850,* 117–122; Weeden, *op. cit.,* II, 837.

2. *Journals of the Congress,* IV, 152–311; Shaw-Perkins Papers, Thomas Shaw to John W. Stanley, January 1783.

3. Noah Webster Papers, MS Diary, December 17, 1784; Shaw-

Perkins Papers, T. Shaw to J. W. Stanley, January 1783, Colonel Jonah Waters to T. Shaw, February 1, 1783.

4. Webster MS Diary, November 29, December 17, 1784; Leon Howard, *The Connecticut Wits,* 3, 160, 169, 171–179, and *passim;* Mary Stoughton Locke, *Anti-Slavery in America,* 92–93; Weeden, *op. cit.,* II, 835.

5. Webster MS Diary, January 29, February 8, 1784.

6. *Ibid.,* March 16, 29, 30, December 17, 1784; Webster Papers, MS "To be inserted after the long answer, Courant, No. 1002"; *Connecticut Courant,* February 24, March 2, 9, 16, April 6, 1784; *Dictionary of American Biography,* XIX, 595; Harry R. Warfel, *Noah Webster, Schoolmaster,* 99ff; John Bach McMaster, *History of the People of the United States,* I, 177–180; Noah Webster, *Sketches of American Policy.*

7. Wolcott Papers, for Wolcott Sr.'s correspondence of 1785–1788 with the Pennsylvania Agricultural Society, in which he espouses the idea of "improvement"; Adams, *New England in the Republic,* 305.

8. Howard, *op. cit.,* 172.

9. Richard J. Purcell, *Connecticut in Transition, 1775–1850,* 174–194; Zephaniah Swift, *A System of Laws of the State of Connecticut,* I, 68, quoted in Noble E. Cunningham Jr., *The Jeffersonian Republicans,* 250; George Gibbs, *Memoirs of the Administrations of Washington and John Adams,* I, *passim;* Adams, *New England in the Republic,* 217–218; Leonard D. White, *The Federalists,* 123–124; *Dictionary of American Biography,* XX, 443–444.

10. Miniature in possession of Robert S. Coit.

11. W. G. Lane Collection (by permission, Yale University Library); Stokes MSS (by permission, Yale University Library), writ of attachment, July 11, 1788, signed by Joshua Coit and Richard Law; *Dictionary of American Biography,* VIII, 10.

12. Lane Collection, August 4, 1785. Cf. John Allen Krout and Dixon Ryan Fox, *The Completion of Independence, 1790–1830 (A History of American Life,* V), 31–32.

13. Brainerd and Coit Papers, John Richards to Coit, August 27, 1796; Labaree, *op. cit.,* VII, 92.

14. Lane Papers, December 28, 1784; Franklin Bowditch Dexter, *Biographical Sketches of the Graduates of Yale College,* IV, 63–64.

15. Coit Papers, quitclaim deed, Amasa Learned to Joshua Coit, September 3, 1789.

16. Connecticut Archives, "Trade and Maritime Affairs, 1668–1789," #174 a-b-c; Labaree, *op. cit.,* V, 431.

17. *Acts and Laws of Connecticut, 1784,* 309–312.

18. Parkhurst, *op. cit.,* VI, 165.

19. Labaree, *op. cit.,* VI, 1–3.

20. *Ibid.,* 3–10.

21. *Acts and Laws of Connecticut, 1785,* 317–323; Labaree, *op. cit.,* VI, 10–35, 37.

22. *Ibid.,* 92; Brainerd and Coit Papers, Coit to Brainerd, May 28, 1785; *Connecticut Courant,* May 30, 1785. This support of indefinite judicial tenure anticipated Judge Zephaniah Swift's proposal for life tenure. Purcell, *op. cit.,* 204.

23. *Connecticut Courant,* May 16, 1785.

24. Labaree, *op. cit.,* VI, 93–103; William Law Learned, *The Learned Family,* 110–111.

25. Brainerd and Coit Papers, Coit to Brainerd, October 18, 1785.

26. *Ibid.*

27. Connecticut Archives, "Ecclesiastical Affairs, 1658–1789," #309; Purcell, *op. cit.,* 12, 48, 81. Extension of toleration to all associations of Christians was finally completed in 1791. Paul Wakeman Coons, *The Achievement of Religious Liberty in Connecticut,* 21–22.

CHAPTER THREE

From Legislature to Congress

1. Joseph Priestley, nonconformist religious liberal and materialist philosopher.

2. Richard Price, clergyman, ethical philosopher, defender of free will, and author of *Observations on the Importance of the American Revolution* (London, 1784).

3. Webster MS Diary, October 14–24, 1786.

4. Connecticut Archives, "Finance and Currency," First Series, V, 223.

5. Blake, *op. cit.,* 538.

6. Labaree, *op. cit.,* VI, 396–398, 469–470, 493–495.

7. *Ibid.,* VII, 3, 369, 475; Connecticut Archives, "Trade and Maritime Affairs, 1668–1789," 248, "Susquehanna Settlers, Western Lands," I, 216.

8. *Ibid.,* "Travel, Highways, etc.," XII, 552–c; Labaree, *op. cit.,* VII, 369; Krout and Fox, *op. cit.,* 79; *Connecticut Gazette,* June 7, 1792; Shaw-Perkins Papers, H. Channing to E. Perkins, May 7, 1793.

9. MSS Joshua Coit to Daniel L. Coit Letters, J. Coit to D. L. Coit, August 26, 1791; Union Bank and Trust Company of New London Archives, MS "Record Book, 1792–1796"; Brainerd and Coit Papers, Coit to Brainerd, May 19, 1792; Webster MS Diary, March 11, 1791, May 28, 1792; State of Connecticut, MS "Records," I, 81; Labaree, *op. cit.,* VII, 388 n, 448–449, 466; Chapman, *op. cit.,* 54–55; *Connecticut Gazette,* June 7, 1782.

10. Union Bank Archives, MS "Record Book, 1792–1796"; State of Connecticut MS "Records," I (1787–1792), 18–20; Coit Papers, MS appraisal of estate of Joshua Coit, November 1798.

11. Labaree, *op. cit.,* VIII, 1 n 2; *Connecticut Courant,* October 14, 1793.

12. MSS Coit Letters to his Wife and Son, May 21, 1793.

13. Cf. Purcell, *op. cit.,* 181–204.

14. Richard H. Shryock, "The Yellow Fever Epidemics, 1793–1905," 51–62.

15. Wolcott Papers, Goodhue to Wolcott Jr., April 15, 1793; Webster Papers, Wolcott Jr. to Webster, August 10, 1793; Shaw-Perkins Papers, H. Channing to [?], May 7, [1793].

16. Jensen, *op. cit.,* 38–39; *Connecticut Gazette,* August 30–November 22, 1792, January 23, February 13, 1794.

17. Adams, *New England in the Republic,* 212–213. Cf. Purcell, *op. cit.,* 210ff, for the aristocratic spirit of Connecticut Federalism, and Krout and Fox, *op. cit.,* 28–46.

18. Dexter, *Diary of Stiles,* III, 502–503; Manning J. Dauer, *The Adams Federalists,* 58–59; Samuel Flagg Bemis, *A Diplomatic History of the United States,* 96–98; Thomas A. Bailey, *Diplomatic History of the American People,* 74–78; Ruhl J. Bartlett, editor, *The Record of American Diplomacy,* 90–91.

19. *Connecticut Courant,* October 21, 1793; Labaree, *op. cit.,* VIII, 84–86, 101–102; *Dictionary of American Biography,* VII, 397.

20. *Connecticut Courant,* November 18, December 9, 1793; Labaree, *op. cit.,* VIII, 96–97 n 19; Gibbs, *op. cit.,* I, 114.

21. MSS Coit Letters, Coit to Mrs. Coit, February 17, March 7, 1794, Coit to Robert C., February 10, March 3, 1794; Wolcott Papers, Wolcott Sr. to Wolcott Jr., December 9, 1793; *Annals of Congress,* Third Congress, First Session, 142; *Connecticut Courant,* November 4, 1793.

22. MSS Joshua Coit to Daniel L. Coit Letters, J. Coit to D. L. Coit, August 27, 1795; Coit Papers, MS Appraisal of Joshua Coit estate.

23. MSS Joshua Coit to Daniel L. Coit Letters, J. Coit to D. L. Coit, January 4, February 6, 1794; *Annals,* Third Congress, First Session, 154, 166, 254–255, 432, 452, 477, 497; Bemis, *op. cit.,* 120.

24. MSS Joshua Coit to Daniel L. Coit Letters, J. Coit to D. L. Coit, March 7, 13, 18, 27, April 8, 10, 16, 1794; *Annals,* Third Congress, First Session, 525–527, 596, 601, 605–606; Gibbs, *op. cit.,* I, 134; Bemis, *op. cit.,* 100–101; Irving Brant, *James Madison, Father of the Constitution, 1787–1800,* 395; Rufus Wilmot Griswold, *The Republican Court or American Society in the Days of Washington,* 301.

25. Gaillard Hunt, *Disunion Sentiment in Congress in 1794,* 11–13, 21–23; Gibbs, *op. cit.,* I, 86; Edward Channing, *A History of the United States,* IV, 155 notes 1 & 2; Charles R. King, *Life and Correspondence of Rufus King,* I, 112–113; Julian P. Boyd, editor, *The Papers of Thomas Jefferson,* X, 276–277, James Monroe to Thomas Jefferson, August 19, 1786; Stanislaus Murry Hamilton, editor, *Writings of James Monroe,* I, 148–151, James Monroe to Governor Patrick Henry, August 12, 1786.

26. MSS Joshua Coit to Daniel L. Coit Letters, J. Coit to D. L. Coit, January 31, February 15, April 22, 26, 1794; MSS Coit Letters, Coit to Mrs. Coit, March 24, 1794.

27. Elias Perkins Papers, Coit to Perkins, April 21, 1794.

28. *Annals,* Third Congress, First Session, 605–606, 715–716.

29. Webster Papers, Wolcott Jr. to Webster, May 3, 1794—which explains Webster's turn to "the defense of conservative principles." Krout and Fox, *op. cit.,* 156.

30. Gibbs, *op. cit.,* I, 135–137.

31. MSS Coit Letters, Coit to Mrs. Coit, March 31, 1794; *The Federalist* #15, 71–72; Cunningham, *op. cit.*, 75.

32. *Annals,* Third Congress, First Session, 667, 709, 723, 758, 779; Wolcott Papers, Goodhue to Wolcott Jr., April 15, 1793.

33. *Connecticut Gazette,* May 22, 1794; Labaree, *op. cit.,* VIII, 193.

CHAPTER FOUR

A Liberal Federalist at Washington's Court

1. Chapman, *op. cit.,* 54–55.

2. Griswold, *op. cit., passim,* for the best account of the "Republican Court"; Morison, *op. cit.,* I, 125–127, 140; Claude G. Bowers, *Jefferson and Hamilton,* 1–18, 116–139.

3. Wolcott Papers, Wolcott Jr. to Webster, May 20, 1793.

4. *Connecticut Gazette,* January 23, February 13, 1794.

5. Wolcott Papers, Wolcott Jr. to Frederic Wolcott, December 15, 1792, quoted in Dumas Malone, *Jefferson and the Rights of Man,* iv; Charles E. Cuningham, *Timothy Dwight, 1752–1817,* 143, 154–158; Dexter, *Diary of Stiles,* III, 247.

6. Dauer, *op. cit.,* 53–70.

7. Morison, *op. cit.,* I, 126–127; Bowers, *op. cit.,* 134, 331–334; Griswold, *op. cit.,* 352–353.

8. William Dunlap, *A History of the American Theatre,* 92–94, 115–117; Henry Wansey, *The Journal of an Excursion to the United States of North America in the Summer of 1794,* 126–127; Paul Leicester Ford, *Washington and the Theatre,* 50; Griswold, *op. cit.,* 313–319.

9. James Thomas Flexner, *American Painting: The Light of Distant Skies, 1760–1835.*

10. Curti, *op. cit.,* 153, 177; Cuningham, *op. cit.,* 171–175 and *passim;* Krout and Fox, *op. cit.,* 178.

11. Flexner, *op. cit.,* 49 and *passim.*

12. MSS Coit Letters, February 19, 1794.

13. *Ibid.,* Coit to Robert C., March 3, 1794; *Connecticut Gazette,* January 19, 1792.

14. MSS Coit Letters, April 22, 1794.

15. *Ibid.,* Coit to Robert C., December 23, 1794.

16. *Ibid.,* February 21, 1794.

17. *Ibid.,* February 28, 1794.

18. *Ibid.,* Coit to Robert C., December 18, 1794; MSS Joshua Coit to Daniel L. Coit Letters, J. Coit to D. L. Coit, April 31, 1794.

19. MSS Coit Letters, Coit to Mrs. Coit, March 24, May 1, 1794. See Frontispiece.

20. *Ibid.,* Coit to Robert C., February 23, 1796.

21. Morison, *op. cit.,* I, 125–127.

22. MSS Joshua Coit to Daniel L. Coit Letters, J. Coit to D. L. Coit, February 20, 1795; MSS Coit Letters, Coit to Mrs. Coit, February 21, 1794, March 2, 7, 1798.

23. *Ibid.,* Coit to Mrs. Coit, February 28, March 18, 31, 1794.

24. *Ibid.,* March 18, 1794. Cf. Krout and Fox, *op. cit.,* 163–166.

25. MSS Coit Letters, Coit to Mrs. Coit, April 22, 1796.

26. *Ibid.,* Coit to Mrs. Coit, March 8, 1796.

27. *Ibid.,* Coit to Mrs. Coit, February 21, 1794.

28. *Ibid.,* Coit to Mrs. Coit, December 6, 1795, February 16, 1796.

29. Coit Papers, deed of October 19, 1796; *Connecticut Gazette,* August 12, 1795; Chapman, *op. cit.,* 60; MSS Joshua Coit to Daniel L. Coit Letters, J. Coit to D. L. Coit, May 1, October 29, 1795, February 12, 1796.

30. *Connecticut Gazette,* July 10, 17, 24, 1794; Adams, *New England in the Republic,* 219; Dexter, *op. cit.,* III, 545–546; Krout and Fox, *op. cit.,* 163–166; Cuningham, *op. cit.,* 299–302.

31. MSS Coit Letters, Coit to Mrs. Coit, December 6, 1794; *Connecticut Gazette,* December 18, 1794; Weaver, *op. cit.,* 25.

32. Henry Channing, *A Discourse Delivered in New-London at the Request of Union Lodge Or Free and Accepted Masons,* 2–27.

33. MSS Coit Letters, correspondence for 1794–1798.

34. *Ibid.;* Perkins Papers, Coit to Perkins, January 2, 22, 1796.

35. MSS Coit Letters.

36. *Ibid.,* Coit to Robert C., May 25, June 23, November 31, 1797, January 13, February 2, April 21, June 11, 16, July 9, 1798.

37. *Ibid.,* Coit to Bulkeley, January 2, 1795, April 17, 1797.

38. Perkins Papers, Coit to Perkins, April 6, 1796.

39. Dauer, *op. cit.,* 72–77.

CHAPTER FIVE
Stability During Crisis

1. Wolcott Papers, Ellsworth to Wolcott Jr., August 20, 1794, Wolcott Jr. to Trench Coxe, September 29, 1794; Edward Channing, *op. cit.*, IV, 138–140; Krout and Fox, *op. cit.*, 100, 160 n 2; Eugene Perry Link, *Democratic-Republican Societies, 1790–1800*, 145–147ff; Hunt, *op. cit.*, 12, 21; McMaster, *op. cit.*, II, 204–206; Raymond Walters Jr., *Albert Gallatin*, 65–86.

2. Perkins Papers, Coit to Perkins, December 2, 1794; *Annals*, Third Congress, Second Session, 931–945; McMaster, *op. cit.*, II, 204–206.

3. Perkins Papers, December 2, 1794.

4. *Ibid.;* MSS Joshua Coit to Daniel L. Coit Letters, J. Coit to D. L. Coit, December 8, 1795.

5. MSS Coit Letters, Coit to Charles Bulkeley, January 2, 1795. This requirement was included in the Act of January 29, 1795.

6. Albert J. Beveridge, *The Life of John Marshall*, III, 546–561; *Annals*, Third Congress, Second Session, 970, 1127, 1131.

7. *Connecticut Courant*, January 18, 1795; *Connecticut Gazette*, January 14, 1795.

8. Perkins Papers, Coit to Perkins, January 22, 1796; *Annals*, Fourth Congress, First Session, 170, 245.

9. *Ibid.*, Third Congress, Second Session, 1219–1222; Perkins Papers, Coit to Perkins, January 26, 1795; Bemis, *op. cit.*, 103; Bailey, *op. cit.*, 64–66.

10. Wolcott Papers, Hopkins to Wolcott Jr., June 28, 1795; Dice Robins Anderson, *William Branch Giles*, 40–43.

11. Wolcott Papers, Webster to Wolcott Jr., July 30, 1795.

12. *Ibid.*, Wolcott Jr. to Goodhue, August 8, 1795; *Connecticut Courant*, July 20, 27, August 17, 24, 1795; Samuel Flagg Bemis, *Jay's Treaty*, 252–271, for analysis of the negotiation and its implications.

13. Wolcott Papers, Jeremiah Wadsworth to Wolcott Jr., January 31, 1796; Dauer, *op. cit.*, 32–33, 289–297.

14. Shaw-Perkins Papers, will of Thomas Shaw, September 25, 1795; *Annals*, Fourth Congress, First Session, 375.

15. Perkins Papers, Coit to Perkins, March 5, 1796.

16. *British Treaty. Debates in the House of Representatives of the United States* . . . Part I, 53–55, 75–76; Gibbs, *op. cit.,* I, 306; *Annals,* Fourth Congress, First Session, 400–401, 426–427. Livingston introduced his resolution on March 2, debate on it began on March 7. Henry Adams, *Life of Albert Gallatin,* 160–163; Brant, *op. cit.,* 434–435.

17. Perkins Papers, Coit to Perkins, March 16, 1796; *Annals,* Fourth Congress, First Session, 654–660; John A. Carroll and Mary W. Ashworth, *George Washington,* VII, *First in Peace,* 350–353.

18. *Annals,* Fourth Congress, First Session, 759; *British Treaty, Debates,* I, 361–362; *Connecticut Gazette,* April 7, 1796; Gibbs, *op. cit.,* I, 323–334.

19. Perkins Papers, Coit to Perkins, March 27, 1796; *British Treaty, Debates,* I, 362.

20. *Ibid.,* I, 363–365; *Annals,* Fourth Congress, First Session, 760–762.

21. Perkins Papers, Coit to Perkins, April 6, 1796.

22. *British Treaty, Debates,* I, 371–372, 374, 386; *Annals,* Fourth Congress, First Session, 771, 783; Cunningham, *op. cit.,* 82–83.

23. *Annals,* Fourth Congress, First Session, 891, 893; Gibbs, *op. cit.,* I, 303–304; Dauer, *op. cit.,* 289–297.

24. Wolcott Papers, Wolcott Jr. to Frederic Wolcott, August 9, 1796; Gibbs, *op. cit.,* I, 327.

25. *Ibid.,* Wm. Moseley to Wolcott Sr., April 24, 1796; *Annals,* Fourth Congress, First Session, 1120–1140; *British Treaty, Debates,* II, 3–28, 145–164.

26. *Ibid.,* II, 207–220; *Annals,* Fourth Congress, First Session, 1140–1153; William B. Hatcher, *Edward Livingston,* 38, 40–41.

27. Bemis, *Jay's Treaty,* 252–271, 322–328.

28. Yale MSS, Uriah Tracy to Tapping Reeve, May 4, 1796; *Annals,* Fourth Congress, First Session, 1291; *British Treaty, Debates,* II, 253, 351–352, 358; *Connecticut Gazette,* May 12, 1796; Gaillard Hunt, editor, *The Writings of James Madison,* VI, 300–301, Madison to James Monroe, May 14, 1796; Brandt, *op. cit.,* 438–439; Carroll and Ashworth, *op. cit.,* 352–353, 364–375.

29. *Connecticut Gazette,* May 26, October 27, 1796; *Connecticut Journal,* October 26, 1796; Gibbs, *op. cit.,* I, 339, 341–342; Samuel H. Fisher, *The Litchfield Law School,* 1775–1833, 2, 21, 25–27.

CHAPTER SIX
Independent Federalist

1. All this is evident in the correspondence between Wolcott Sr. and Wolcott Jr., 1794–1797, in Gibbs, *op. cit.;* Hunt, *op. cit.;* the "Pelham" essays in the *Connecticut Courant,* November 21, December 12, 1796, and in 1798; the "Gustavus" essays in *ibid.,* during 1797–1798; and Wolcott Papers, Dr. L. Hopkins to Wolcott Jr., August 3, 1790, June 28, 1795, Wolcott Jr. to Noah Webster, August 1, 1795, Wolcott Jr. to Goodhue, August 8, 1795.

2. Gibbs, *op. cit.,* I, 322–323; Anderson, *op. cit.,* 49–50.

3. Purcell, *op. cit.,* 17–30, 301, 310; Cuningham, *op. cit.,* 293–301, 315–329; Adams, *New England in the Republic,* 218–220.

4. Alexander DeConde, "Washington's Farewell, the French Alliance, and the Election of 1796," 643.

5. *Ibid.,* 653–656; Wolcott Papers, Wolcott Jr. to Alexander Hamilton, November 7, 1796, Hamilton to Wolcott Jr., November 22, 1796, Fisher Ames to Wolcott Jr., November 14, 1796, Wolcott Sr. to Wolcott Jr., November 21, 1796; Gibbs, *op. cit.,* I, 396–397.

6. Channing, *op. cit.,* IV, 75–76, 154–156; Beveridge, *op. cit.,* I, 250, 255–264, III, 5 n; Krout and Fox, *op. cit.,* 74–75, 185; Adams, *op. cit.,* 186–187, 190.

7. After the close of the Napoleonic Era and the disappearance of serious external danger, sectionalism suddenly challenged nationalism in the United States despite the Industrial Revolution.

8. DeConde, *op. cit.,* 647–648.

9. *Ibid.,* 656; Wolcott Papers, Wolcott Sr. to Wolcott Jr., November 27, 1796.

10. DeConde, *op. cit.,* 656–657; Cunningham, *op. cit.,* 101.

11. Wolcott Papers, Wolcott Sr. to Wolcott Jr., November 21, 28, 1796; *Connecticut Courant,* November 21, December 12, 1796.

12. Wolcott Papers, Wolcott Jr. to Wolcott Sr., November 15, 19, 27, 1796, Fisher Ames to Wolcott Jr., November 14, 1796, George Cabot to Wolcott Jr., November 30, 1796, etc. Cf. Dauer, *op. cit.,* 97–101, for a different estimate of Wolcott Jr.'s position.

13. Wolcott Papers, Wolcott Sr. to Wolcott Jr., December 12, 1796,

Cabot to Wolcott Jr., April 3, 1797; *Connecticut Courant,* December 15, 26, 1796; Dauer, *op. cit.,* 106; *Connecticut Journal* (New Haven), November 9, 1796.

14. Perkins Papers.

15. *Ibid.*

16. Jeremiah Wadsworth Papers, Coit to Wadsworth, February 17, 1797; Wolcott Papers, Chauncey Goodrich to Wolcott Sr., February 10, 1797, Wolcott Jr. to John Fitzgerald, March 29, 1797; *Connecticut Gazette,* February 2, 16, 1797. This analysis revises White, *op. cit.,* 514, regarding "the moral standards of the Federalist public service."

17. *Ibid.,* April 3, May 15, 22, June 12, 19, 1797; *Annals,* Fifth Congress, First Session, 50, 60–63, 68–70, 135–136, 193–201, 209–210, 230–234; *Connecticut Gazette,* May 25, June 8, 1797.

18. Wolcott Papers, March 31, 1797; *Connecticut Courant,* May 15, June 12, 1797.

19. Wolcott Papers, March 27, 1797.

20. *Ibid.,* Goodrich to Wolcott Sr., May 20, 1797; *Annals,* Fifth Congress, First Session, 239; Howard R. Marraro, "The Four Versions of Jefferson's Letter to Mazzei," 18–29; Dauer, *op. cit.,* 128–129; Bernard Mayo, *Jefferson Himself,* 198.

21. George Cabot, leader of the Essex Junto, asserted to Wolcott Jr., May 24, 1797, Wolcott Papers, that President Adams' message to Congress was "in itself the most truly national" and that it would excite "the *most national feeling* of any thing that has been publicized since the French disease infected our country." Cf. Channing, *op. cit.,* IV, 179–181; Dauer, *op. cit.,* 4–23, 32–33, 127–128.

22. *Annals,* Fifth Congress, First Session, 257, 280–281, 297, 323–324, 347, 349–352, 355–356, 374, 376–378, 409; Dauer, *op. cit.,* 298–303; *Columbian Centinel,* July 1, 1797.

23. *Annals,* Fifth Congress, First Session, 369–370, 377.

24. *Ibid.,* 385–386; *Connecticut Courant,* July 10, 1797; *Columbian Centinel,* July 1, 1797; Dauer, *op. cit.,* 133–136.

25. *Ibid.,* 66, 102, and *passim;* Channing, *op. cit.,* IV, 236.

26. Wolcott Papers, Coit to Wolcott Jr., June 26, 1797. Italics added.

27. *Annals,* Fifth Congress, First Session, 389, 391, 394–395, 398, 400, 446–447.

28. *Columbian Centinel,* July 12, August 2, 5, 1797; *The Weekly Oracle,* July 8, 1797.

29. *The Bee,* September 13, 1797; *Connecticut Courant,* September 4, 1797.

30. MSS Coit Letters, Coit to Robert C., February 7, May 25, June 23, 1797.

CHAPTER SEVEN
Prelude to Crisis

1. Dauer, *op. cit.,* 142 and *passim.*

2. *Ibid.,* 142; *Connecticut Gazette,* November 29, 1797; *Annals,* Fifth Congress, Second Session, 627. Goodrich's reports to Governor Wolcott Sr. do not mention Coit. Gibbs, *op. cit.,* I, *passim.*

3. *Annals,* Fifth Congress, Second Session, 625, 627, 892, 942, 1090; Dauer, *op. cit.,* 137–139.

4. MSS Coit Letters, February 11, 1798.

5. *Annals,* Fifth Congress, Second Session, 628, 1243; *Country Porcupine,* March 9, 1798; *Middlesex Gazette,* December 1, 1797; *Connecticut Gazette,* November 29, 1797.

6. *Annals,* Fifth Congress, Second Session, 636, 644–645, 701, 710, 786–788; *Middlesex Gazette,* December 8, 22, 1797; *Connecticut Gazette,* December 20, 1797; Morison, *op. cit.,* I, 149.

7. *Annals,* Fifth Congress, Second Session, 777–778, 789, 798, 807–809.

8. Coit was second on the list after Hillhouse and Tracy, who were already United States Senators. *Connecticut Gazette,* December 27, 1797; *The Bee,* November 25, 1797.

9. Cuningham, *op. cit.,* opposite 316; Krout and Fox, *op. cit.,* 166.

10. MSS Coit Letters, Coit to Mrs. Coit, February 11, 15, 1798; Harrison Gray Otis Papers, H. G. Otis to Mrs. Otis, February 7, 14, 1798; *Annals,* Fifth Congress, Second Session, 955–959, 961–963, 966–967, 972–974, 981–982, 1002, 1008–1029; *Connecticut Courant,* February 12, 19, 26, March 5, 19, 1798; *Connecticut Journal,* February 15, 22, 1798; *Report of the Committee of Privileges . . . ,* 4.

11. Theodore Sedgwick Papers, Coit to Sedgwick, February 11, 1798; *Connecticut Courant,* February 19, 26, March 5, 1798. "Plain Truth" declared on February 26 that "Decus" was "an intemperate partisan." Cf. Perkins Papers, Coit to Perkins, March 8, 1798.

12. Morison, *op. cit.,* I, 87, Jonathan Mason Jr. to Otis, February 19, 1798.

13. Otis Papers, Otis to Mrs. Otis, February 7, 14, 1798; *Annals,* Fifth Congress, Second Session, 1036–1043, 1058–1059, 1063–1068; *Connecticut Courant,* February 26, 1798; *Middlesex Gazette,* February 23, 1798; *The Bee,* February 28, 1798.

14. MSS Coit Letters, February 15, 1798; Adams, *Gallatin,* 191; Hunt, *Writings of Madison,* VI, 310–311, Madison to Jefferson, February 1798.

15. *Connecticut Courant,* March 12, 1798.

16. MSS Coit Letters, Coit to Mrs. Coit, March 8, 1798; Perkins Papers, Coit to Perkins, March 8, 1798.

17. Supra, p. 102.

18. MSS Coit Letters, March 2, 1798.

19. *Annals,* Fifth Congress, Second Session, 1070, 1083, 1098; *Connecticut Courant,* March 12, 1798; *The Bee,* March 14, 1798.

20. Otis Papers, Otis to Mrs. Otis, March 8, 1798.

21. *Annals,* Fifth Congress, Second Session, 1098–1101, 1234; *Connecticut Courant,* March 12, 19, 1798; Dauer, *op. cit.,* 140, 304–310.

22. MSS Coit Letters, March 8, 1798.

23. Otis Papers, Otis to Mrs. Otis, March 17, 1798; Adams, *Gallatin,* 197–198.

24. *Annals,* Fifth Congress, Second Session, 1249–1252; *Connecticut Courant,* March 26, April 30, 1798; Perkins Papers, Perkins to Coit, March 26, 1798.

CHAPTER EIGHT

The French War and Civil Liberties

1. Beveridge, *op. cit.,* II, 335; Crane Brinton, *The Lives of Talleyrand,* 106–109.

2. Dauer, *op. cit.,* 142–143, 145–146.

3. *Annals,* Fifth Congress, Second Session, 1358–1359, 1369–1371.

4. Beveridge, *op. cit.,* II, 337–356; Dauer, *op. cit.,* 141–143; Channing, *op. cit.,* IV, 189; Bemis, *Diplomatic History,* 117; Gilbert Chinard, *Thomas Jefferson: The Apostle of Americanism,* 337; Morison, *op. cit.,* I, 140; Walters, *op. cit.,* 106–107.

5. Italics added. *Annals,* Fifth Congress, Second Session, 1319; *Connecticut Journal,* April 12, 1798; Cunningham, *op. cit.,* 125.

6. MSS Joshua Coit to Daniel L. Coit Letters, J. Coit to D. L. Coit, April 8, 1798; Wolcott Papers, Wolcott to Hamilton, April 5, 1798; Dauer, *op. cit.,* 150–151.

7. *Ibid.,* 146–147.

8. Wolcott Papers, Higginson to Wolcott, June 29, 1798, *et seq.* for the former's detection of Talleyrand's communications with the Republican leader; Morison, *op. cit.,* 150–151; Walters, *op. cit.,* 107.

9. Morison, *op. cit.,* 140–147.

10. Dauer, *op. cit.,* 147, 149.

11. *Annals,* Fifth Congress, Second Session, 1402, 1425–1426, 1815–1835, 1954; *Connecticut Courant,* June 4, 1798; *The Bee,* June 6, 1798; *Middlesex Gazette,* May 25, 1798. According to *Porcupine Gazette,* April 3, 1798, America should depend upon British convoys in a war with France. Dauer, *op. cit.,* 149. This may explain Coit's vote for reduction in the number of sloops of war. Walters, *op. cit.,* 108–109.

12. *Annals,* Fifth Congress, Second Session, 1858–1867, 1874–1875, 1925, 2056–2066; *Country Porcupine,* June 2–4, 14–15, 1798; *Connecticut Courant,* June 12, July 9, 1798.

13. *Ibid.,* July 16, 23, 1798; *Annals,* Fifth Congress, Second Session, 1858, 2092–2094, 2127–2128, 2132; *Country Porcupine,* July 7–9, 1798.

14. MSS Coit Letters, Coit to Mrs. Coit, April 22, 1798, Coit to Robert C., May 11, 1798.

15. MSS Joshua Coit to Daniel L. Coit Letters, J. Coit to D. L. Coit, June 12, 1798; *Annals,* Fifth Congress, Second Session, 1878–1890; *Connecticut Courant,* June 18, 1798; *Connecticut Gazette,* June 20, 1798.

16. Timothy Pickering Papers, Pickering to Rufus King, July 9, 17, 1798; *Annals,* Fifth Congress, Second Session, 2181; *Connecticut Courant,* July 23, 1798; John Spencer Bassett, *The Federalist System, 1789–1801,* 237.

17. James Thompson Callender, Virginia Republican journalist.

18. *Country Porcupine,* June 9–11, 1798.

19. Italics added. MSS Coit Papers.

20. *Ibid.,* July 9, 1798.

21. Wolcott Papers; Otis Papers, J. Mason Jr. to H. G. Otis, May 28, 1798, which expresses the war faction's demand for war with France; Pickering Papers, F. Ames to Pickering, June 4, 1798, Hamilton to Pickering, June 8, 1798, S. Higginson to Pickering, June 9, 1798, Timothy Pickering to John Pickering Jr., June 15, 1798; Gibbs, *op. cit.,* II, 70–71; *Middlesex Gazette,* June 22, 1798.

22. Wolcott Papers, Higginson to Wolcott, June 29, 1798; Jefferson's *Anas,* quoted in Morison, *Otis,* I, 97–98; Dauer, *op. cit.,* 168–170.

23. *Middlesex Gazette,* April 20, 27, 1798.

24. Cf. MS Order Book of Captain Stephen Peabody, 1799–1800 (by permission of John G. Howe, Jr., Albion, Michigan); Channing, *op. cit.,* IV, 196–200.

25. *Connecticut Courant,* April–July 1798; Shaw-Perkins Papers, E. D. Williams to Perkins, March 19, 1798.

26. Channing, *op. cit.,* IV, 198–199, for the exchange of sailing signals between the American and British navies during the Naval War.

27. *Ibid.,* 219–220; Dauer, *op. cit.,* 157–159; Gibbs, *op. cit.,* I, 136; James Morton Smith, *Freedom's Fetters: The Alien and Sedition Laws and American Civil Liberties,* 21, 23–24, 26; John Holland Rose, *Life of William Pitt,* II, 286–287, 333; Adams, *New England in the Republic,* 224–226.

28. Smith, *op. cit.,* 26, quoting Jefferson to Madison, April 26, 1798; Dauer, *op. cit.,* 152; Adams, *Gallatin,* 202; *Annals,* Fifth Congress, Second Session, 1427.

29. *Ibid.,* 1453–1454; *Connecticut Courant,* April 30, 1798; Dauer, *op. cit.,* 153; Smith, *op. cit.,* 26.

30. *Ibid.,* 22–23, 27–28; *Annals,* Fifth Congress, Second Session, 1630–1631, 1776–1783.

31. *Ibid.,* 1566–1570, 1630–1631, 1776–1783, 1785–2039; *The Bee,* May 23, 1798, quoting the *Aurora; Country Porcupine,* June 21–22, 1798; Dauer, *op. cit.,* 152–159; John C. Miller, *Crisis in Freedom. The Alien*

and *Sedition Acts,* 50–53; Smith, *op. cit.,* 22–39, 47–59; Hatcher, *op. cit.,* 47.

32. *Ibid.,* 107; Miller, *op. cit.,* 47–49; *Annals,* Fifth Congress, Second Session, 1482.

33. *Ibid.,* 2093–2114; *The Bee,* July 18, 1798; Miller, *op. cit.,* 161–165; Smith, *op. cit.,* 128–132, 143–145.

34. Cf. Dauer, *op. cit.,* 165–260; Smith, *op. cit.,* 160ff. But Channing, *op. cit.,* IV, 217–237, argues that the Presidential victory of the Republicans derived exclusively from their success in electing a slate of Republican assemblymen from New York City. However, the revival of the Republican Party during 1799–1800 can be attributed largely to the factors mentioned *and* to the Federalists' revenue program arising from heavier armaments, whose effect upon the political affiliation of commercial farming Congressional districts gave the Republicans control of Congress. This has been carefully analyzed by Dauer. Cf. Cunningham, *op. cit.,* 248.

35. *The Bee,* June 20, July 11, 1798.

CHAPTER NINE
An Untimely Exit

1. *Connecticut Journal,* December 28, 1797, May 23, 1798; *Connecticut Courant,* April 9, May 21, June 11, 1798. Cf. *ibid.,* May 21, 1798, for Coit-Griswold correspondence.

2. MSS Coit Letters.

3. Charles Holt, *A Short Account of Yellow-Fever as It Appeared in New-London, in August, September, and October, 1798,* 2–5 and *passim.*

4. *Ibid.,* pp. 5–6, 11. For the earliest reports of Coit's death, *Connecticut Gazette,* September 5, 1798; *Connecticut Courant,* September 10, 1798.

5. Chapman, *op. cit.,* 59.

6. Henry Adams, *History of the United States during the Administrations of Thomas Jefferson and James Madison,* II, 160–191.

7. Coit Papers, Coit to [?], January 5, 1798, enclosing undated will which Coit later dated July 4, 1798, MS Court of Probate order, November 19, 1798, and MS appraisal of estate of Joshua Coit, Esq.

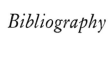

Bibliography

Brainerd, Jeremiah Gates, and Coit, Joshua, Attorneys, 1779–1863, Papers. Connecticut State Library.

Coit, Joshua, Letters to His Wife and Son Robert. Courtesy of Miss Gertrude E. Coit, New London, Connecticut.

Coit, Joshua, Letters to Daniel Lathrop Coit of Norwich, Connecticut, 1779–1798. Courtesy of Robert Sumner Coit, Cambridge, Massachusetts.

Coit, Joshua, Papers. New London County Historical Society.

Connecticut Archives. Connecticut State Library.

First Church of Christ, Congregational, New London, Archives.

Harvard University Archives. Harvard University Library.

Journals of the House, &c., and of the State Convention. Connecticut State Library.

Lane, W. G., Collection. Yale University Library.

Order Book of Captain Stephen Peabody, 1799–1800. Courtesy of John G. Howe Jr., Albion, Michigan.

Otis, Harrison Gray, Papers. Massachusetts Historical Society.

Perkins, Elias, Papers. New London County Historical Society.

Pickering, Timothy, Papers. Massachusetts Historical Society.

Sedgwick, Theodore, Papers. Massachusetts Historical Society.

Shaw-Perkins Papers. New London County Historical Society.

Stokes Manuscripts. Yale University Library.

Union Bank and Trust Company of New London Archives, New London, Connecticut. Courtesy of President Joseph A. Stanners.

Wadsworth, Jeremiah, Papers. Connecticut Historical Society.

Webster, Noah, Papers. New York Public Library.

Wolcott Jr., Oliver, Papers. Connecticut Historical Society.

Yale University Miscellaneous Manuscripts. Yale University Library.

PUBLISHED SOURCE MATERIALS

Acts and Laws of the State of Connecticut in America (New London, 1784, 1785, etc.).

Adams, Henry, editor. *The Writings of Albert Gallatin* (three volumes, Philadelphia, 1879).

Annals of Congress (Washington, 1923).

The Bee (New London), 1797–1798.

Boyd, Julian P., editor. *The Papers of Thomas Jefferson,* I–XIII (Princeton, 1954–1956).

British Treaty. Debates in the House of Representatives of the United States, during the First Session of the Fourth Congress, Upon Questions Involved in the British Treaty of 1794 (two parts, second edition, Philadelphia, 1808).

Catalogus Eorum qui in Collegio Harvardino, quod est Cantabrigiae Nov-Anglorum ab Anno MDCXLII, ad annum MDCCLXXVI, alicujus Gradus Laurea donati sunt (Boston, MDCCLXXVI).

Channing, Henry. *A Discourse Delivered in New-London at the Request of Union Lodge Or Free and Accepted Masons: On The Anniversary of St. John the Baptist, June 30, 1796* (New London, 1796).

Columbian Centinel (Boston), 1797.

Connecticut Courant (Hartford), 1784–1798.

Connecticut Gazette (New London), 1792–1798.

Connecticut Journal (New Haven), 1796–1798.

Country Porcupine (Philadelphia), 1798.

Dexter, Franklin, editor. *The Literary Diary of Ezra Stiles, President of Yale College* (three volumes, New York, 1901).

Gazette of the United States (Philadelphia), 1793–1798.

Hamilton, Alexander; Madison, James; and Jay, John. *The Federalist* (London, Everyman's Library, 1911).

Hamilton, Stanislaus Murry, editor. *Writings of James Monroe* (seven volumes, New York, 1898).

Hempstead, Joshua. *Diary of Joshua Hempstead of New London, Connecticut, September, 1711, to November, 1758* (New London County Historical Society, *Collections,* I) (New London, 1901).

Hoadley, Charles J.; Labaree, Leonard Woods; Fennelly, Catherine; and Van Dusen, Albert E. *Records of the State of Connecticut,* I–IX (Hartford, 1894–1953).

Holt, Charles. *A Short Account of Yellow Fever as It Appeared in New-London, in August, September, and October, 1798* (New London, 1798).

Hunt, Gaillard, editor. *Disunionist Sentiment in Congress in 1794. A Confidential Memorandum Hitherto Unpublished Written by John Taylor of Caroline Senator from Virginia for James Madison* (Washington, 1905).

———. *The Writings of James Madison* (ten volumes, New York, 1906).

Journals of the Congress, IV (Washington, 1823).

Lane, William Coolidge, editor. *Letters of Nathaniel Walker Appleton to His Classmate Eliphalet Pearson, 1773–1784* [reprint from *The Publications of the Colonial Society of Massachusetts,* VII (Cambridge, 1906), 291–306].

Middlesex Gazette (Middletown), 1794–1798.

Porcupine Gazette (Philadelphia), 1798.

Report of the Committee of Privileges, to whom was referred, on the thirtieth ultimo, A Motion Relative to the "expulsion from the House, of Matthew Lyon, for a gross indecency committed upon the person of Roger Griswold, a member from Connecticut, in the presence of the House, while sitting. 2 February, 1798 [Philadelphia, 1798].

Wansey, Henry. *The Journal of an Excursion to the United States of North America in the Summer of 1794* (London, 1796).

Warfel, Henry R., editor. *Letters of Noah Webster* (New York, 1953).

The Weekly Oracle (New London), 1796–1797.

SECONDARY AUTHORITIES

Adams, Henry. *History of the United States during the Administrations of Thomas Jefferson and James Madison, 1801–1817* (nine volumes, New York, 1890).

———. *Life of Albert Gallatin* (Philadelphia, 1889).

Adams, James Truslow. *Revolutionary New England, 1691–1776* (Boston, 1923).

————. *New England in the Republic, 1776–1850* (Boston, 1926).

Allyn, Charles. *The Battle of Groton Heights: A Collection of Narratives, Official Reports, Records, etc. of the Storming of Fort Griswold . . . on the Sixth of September, 1781* (New London, 1882).

Anderson, Dice Robins. *William Branch Giles* (Menasha, 1914).

Bailey, Thomas A. *Diplomatic History of the American People* (fourth edition, New York, 1950).

Bartlett, Ruhl J., editor. *The Record of American Diplomacy* (second edition, New York, 1950).

Bassett, John Spencer. *The Federalist System, 1789–1801 (The American Nation,* XI) (New York, 1906).

Bemis, Samuel Flagg. *A Diplomatic History of the United States* (third edition, New York, 1950).

————. *Jay's Treaty* (New York, 1923).

Beveridge, Albert J. *The Life of John Marshall* (four volumes, Boston, 1919).

Blake, S. Leroy. *Later History of the First Church of New London, Conn.* (New London, 1900).

Bowers, Claude G. *Jefferson and Hamilton: The Struggle for Democracy in America* (Boston, 1925).

Boyd, Julian Parks. *The Susquehanna Company: Connecticut's Experiment in Expansion* (New Haven, 1935).

Brant, Irving. *James Madison, Father of the Constitution, 1787–1800* (Indianapolis and New York, 1950).

Brinton, Crane. *The Lives of Talleyrand* (New York, 1936).

Brown, Charles Raymond. *The Northern Confederacy according to the Plans of the "Essex Junto" 1796–1814* (Princeton, 1915).

Carroll, John Alexander, and Ashworth, Mary Wells. *George Washington,* VII, *First in Peace* (New York, 1957).

Caukins, Frances Manwaring. *History of New London, Connecticut, From the First Survey of the Coast in 1612 to 1860* (New London, 1895).

————. *History of Norwich, Connecticut, from its Settlement in 1660 to January 1845* (Norwich, 1845).

Channing, Edward. *A History of the United States* (six volumes, New York, 1905–1925).

Chapman, Reverend F. W. *The Coit Family; or the Descendants of John Coit* (Hartford, 1874).

Chinard, Gilbert. *Thomas Jefferson: The Apostle of Americanism* (Boston, 1946).

Coons, Paul Wakeman. *The Achievement of Religious Liberty in Connecticut* (New Haven, 1936).

Cuningham, Charles E. *Timothy Dwight, 1752–1817* (New York, 1942).

Cunningham, Noble E., Jr. *The Jeffersonian Republicans, The Formation of Party Organization, 1789–1801* (Chapel Hill, 1956).

Curti, Merle. *The Growth of American Thought* (revised edition, New York, 1951).

Dauer, Manning J. *The Adams Federalists* (Baltimore, 1953).

DeConde, Alexander. "Washington's Farewell, the French Alliance, and the Election of 1796," *Mississippi Valley Historical Review*, XLIII (March, 1957), 641–658.

Dexter, Franklin Bowditch. *Biographical Sketches of the Graduates of Yale College with Annals of the College History*, IV, *July, 1778–June, 1792* (New York, 1907).

Dictionary of American Biography (twenty volumes, New York, 1936).

Dodd, William E. *The Life of Nathaniel Macon* (Raleigh, 1903).

Dunlap, William. *A History of the American Theatre* (New York, 1832).

Eliot, Samuel A. *A Sketch of the History of Harvard College and of its Present State* (Boston, 1848).

Fisher, Samuel H. *The Litchfield Law School, 1775–1831* (New Haven, 1933).

Flexner, James Thomas. *American Painting: The Light of Distant Skies, 1760–1836* (New York, 1954).

Ford, Emily Ellsworth Fowler, compiler. *Notes on the Life of Noah Webster* (two volumes, New York, 1912).

Ford, Paul Leicester. *Washington and the Theatre* (New York, 1899).

Gibbs, George, editor. *Memoirs of the Administrations of Washington and John Adams. Edited from the Papers of Oliver Wolcott, Secretary of the Treasury* (two volumes, New York, 1846).

Griswold, Rufus Wilmot. *The Republican Court or American Society in the Days of Washington* (New York, 1856, 1867).

Hatcher, William B. *Edward Livingston* (University, La., 1940).

Howard, Leon. *The Connecticut Wits* (Chicago, 1943).

Hurd, D. Hamilton. *History of New London County, Connecticut, with Biographical Sketches of Many of Its Pioneers and Prominent Men* (Philadelphia, 1882).

Jensen, Merrill. *The Articles of Confederation* (Madison, 1940).

King, Charles R. *The Life and Correspondence of Rufus King* (seven volumes, New York, 1894).

Krout, John Allen, and Fox, Dixon Ryan. *The Completion of Independence, 1790–1830* (*A History of American Life,* V) (New York, 1944).

Kurtz, Stephen G. *The Presidency of John Adams, The Collapse of Federalism, 1795–1800* (Philadelphia, 1957).

Learned, William Law, compiler. *The Learned Family being Descendants of William Learned* (Albany, 1898).

Link, Eugene Perry. *Democratic-Republican Societies, 1790–1800* (New York, 1942).

Locke, Mary Stoughton. *Anti-Slavery in America from the Introduction of African Slaves to the Prohibition of the Slave Trade (1619–1808)* (Boston, 1901).

Lodge, Henry Cabot. *Life and Letters of George Cabot* (Boston, 1877).

McLaughlin, J. Fairfax. *Matthew Lyon: The Hampden of Congress* (New York, 1900).

McMaster, John Bach. *History of the People of the United States* (eight volumes, New York, 1883–1913).

Malone, Dumas. *Jefferson and His Times.* II, *Jefferson and the Rights of Man* (Boston, 1951).

Marraro, Howard R. "The Four Versions of Jefferson's Letter to Mazzei," *William and Mary Quarterly,* Series II, Volume XXII (Williamsburg, January, 1942), 18–29.

Mayo, Bernard. *Jefferson Himself* (Boston, 1942).

Miller, John C. *Crisis in Freedom: The Alien and Sedition Acts* (Boston, 1951).

Mitchell, Mary Hewitt. *The Great Awakening and Other Revivals in the Religious Life of Connecticut* (New Haven, 1934).

Morgan, Edmund S. *The Birth of the Republic, 1763–1789* (Chicago, 1956).

Morison, Samuel Eliot. *The Life and Letters of Harrison Gray Otis, Federalist, 1765–1848* (two volumes, Boston, 1913).
——. *Three Centuries of Harvard, 1636–1936* (Cambridge, 1932).
Morse, Jarvis Means. *Connecticut Newspapers in the Eighteenth Century* (New Haven, 1936).
Parkhurst, Charles Dyer, compiler. *New London, Connecticut and Vicinity. Early Families*, VI (Hartford, 1938).
Perkins, Mary E. *Old Houses of the Antient Town of Norwich, 1660–1800* (Norwich, 1895).
Purcell, Richard J. *Connecticut in Transition, 1775–1818* (Washington, 1918).
Rogers, Ernest E. *Connecticut Naval Office at New London during the War of the American Revolution* (New London County Historical Society *Collections,* II) (New London, 1933).
Rose, John Holland. *Life of William Pitt* (two volumes, New York, 1924).
Schlesinger, Arthur Meier. *The Colonial Merchants and the American Revolution, 1763–1776* (New York, 1918).
Shryock, Richard H., "The Yellow Fever Epidemics, 1793–1905," in Daniel Aaron, editor, *America in Crisis* (New York, 1952), 50–70.
Smith, J. Eugene. *One Hundred Years of Hartford's Courant From Colonial Times Through the Civil War* (New Haven, 1949).
Smith, James Morton. *Freedom's Fetters: The Alien and Sedition Laws and American Civil Liberties* (Ithaca, 1956).
Van Dusen, Albert E. *Connecticut* (New York, 1961).
Warfel, Harry R. *Noah Webster, Schoolmaster to America* (New York, 1936).
Walters, Raymond, Jr. *Albert Gallatin* (New York, 1957).
Weaver, Glenn. *Jonathan Trumbull, Connecticut's Merchant Magistrate (1710–1785)* (Hartford, 1955).
Webster, Noah. *Sketches of American Policy* (Hartford, 1785).
Weeden, William B. *Economic and Social History of New England, 1620–1789* (two volumes, Boston, 1891).
Welling, James C. *Connecticut Federalism or Aristocratic Politics in a Social Democracy* (New York, 1890).
White, Leonard D. *The Federalists. A Study in Administrative History* (New York, 1948).

Index